Woman's Day.
PASTA
AND GRAINS

Sedgewood® Press

New York

Photographer Credits

Ben Calvo: pages 13, 15, 18, 25, 33, 39, 43, 45, 46, 51 59, 62, 66, 70, 82, 83, 84, 85, 86 (both), 105, 116, 119, 126
Katrina Filary: page 118
Bruce Lemerise: page 117
Michael Molkinthin: page 38
Stephen Mark Neebham: page 44
Joe Standart: pages 4, 36, 57, 90, 94, 96, 97
Ben Swedowsky: pages 60, 78
Mark Thomas: page 12
Eleanor Thompson: page 79
Tim Turner: page 100
John Uher: pages 8, 23, 28, 30, 42, 48, 52, 54, 63, 65, 76, 81, 89, 99, 102, 103, 106, 110, 112, 123, 124

Please address your correspondence to
Customer Service Department, Sedgewood® Press,
Meredith Corporation,
150 East 52nd Street, New York, NY 10022.

For Diamandis Communications Inc.

Editor-in-Chief, *Woman's Day:* Ellen R. Levine
Food Editor: Elizabeth Alston
Researchers: Mary Rieger, Marinella Cancio

For Sedgewood® Press

Director: Elizabeth P. Rice
Editorial Director: Alison Brown Cerier
Project Editor: Miriam Rubin
Copyeditor: Joan Michel
Designer: Remo Cosentino
Production Manager: Bill Rose

The following material was adapted from previously published books and is used by permission of the publishers:

Japanese Cold Thin Noodles (Cold Thin Noodles) from *At Home with Japanese Cooking* by Elizabeth Andoh. Copyright © 1974, 1975, 1980 by Elizabeth Andoh. Reprinted by permission of Alfred A. Knopf Inc.

Macaroni with Beans, Pastitsio for a Party, Spaghetti Carbonara, Swordfish-Olive Pasta from *Beard on Pasta* by James Beard. Copyright © 1983 by James Beard. Reprinted by permission of Alfred A. Knopf Inc.

Shells and Tuna Sauce from *The Fine Art of Italian Cooking* by Giuliano Bugialli. Copyright © 1977 by Giuliano Bugialli. Reprinted by permission of Times Books, a division of Random House Inc.

Vermicelli with Onions Oriental. Adapted from *The Pasta Salad Book* by Nina Graybill and Maxine Rapoport. Copyright © 1984 by Nina Graybill and Maxine Rapoport. Reprinted with permission of Farragut Publishing Co., Inc.

Whole-Wheat Pasta with Grilled-Tomato Sauce from *Chez Panisse Pasta, Pizza and Calzone* by Alice Waters, Patricia Curtan and Martine Labro. Copyright © 1984 by Tango Rose, Inc. Reprinted by permission of Random House Inc.

Contents

RECIPE SYMBOLS

At the beginning of many recipes are symbols pointing out which dishes are:

♥ **LOW-CALORIE** (main-dish serving under 300 calories)

◷ **MAKE-AHEAD** (part or all of the recipe can or should be made ahead)

✳ **MICROWAVE** (recipe or variation)

★ **SPECIAL—AND WORTH IT** (in terms of time, calories or expense)

Pasta with Vegetables

Vegetables are a natural companion to pasta—in a simple tomato sauce or a garden-fresh medley, or with cheese and beans in a hearty vegetarian dish.

Confetti Pasta

Pasta Shapes

High-quality pasta is made from semolina, a form of durum wheat and water (and, if enriched, B vitamins and iron). Pasta is low in fat and sodium and high in complex carbohydrates. Five ounces cooked (2 ounces dry) contain only 210 calories and 1 gram of fat. Store uncooked dry pasta up to one year in covered containers in a cool, dry place.

☐ Pasta comes in over 150 shapes and sizes. Give a pasta dish a new twist by trying a different shape.

Even spaghetti varies from very thin vermicelli and capellini to medium spaghettini and thicker spaghetti. Shapes run from straight solid rods to slightly flattened and narrow linguine or thick, wavy fusilli.

☐ Macaroni is tubular and comes in long pierced strands (such as perciatelli), short curved or straight lengths, plus shells, elbows, ziti and the thicker rigatoni.

☐ Noodles are flat and made with eggs. Green varieties contain dried spinach. Noodles are cut in different lengths and come in various thicknesses and widths. The small flat ribbons called fettuccine are less than ½ inch wide. Although lasagne is sometimes called a noodle, it contains no eggs.

Matching the Pasta to the Sauce

☐ Thin spaghetti and linguine are good with milder sauces, such as clam or tuna. The slender strands provide greater surface area for the sauce to cling to, so there is more sauce per mouthful.

☐ Thicker cuts, such as ziti and rotelle, are sturdy enough to carry sauces heavy with beans, meat or vegetables.

☐ Hollow shapes and spiral twists are good choices for sauces with small bits of meat and vegetables because they catch morsels in their crevices and cavities.

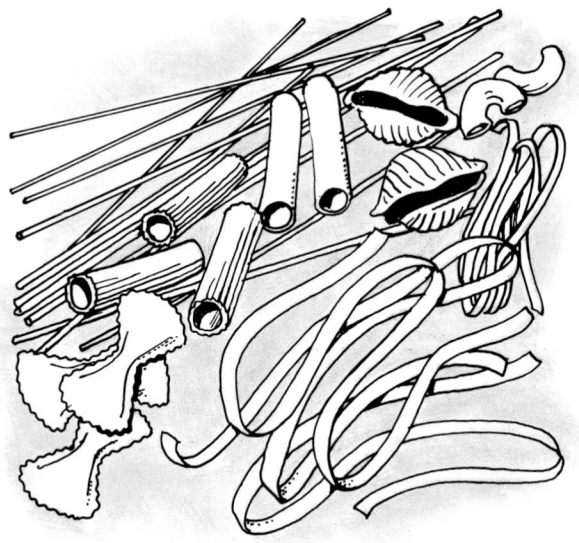

☐ Manicotti, macaroni, rigatoni, lasagne and shells are the best shapes for baking and stuffing.

☐ Rotini, radiatore (named after radiators), seashells and farfalle (bow ties) are good choices for salads. They stand up to assertive dressings and tangy seasonings.

How Much Pasta?

☐ Most dry pasta doubles in volume when cooked. For accuracy, measure uncooked pasta by weight rather than cup. Cooked pasta can be measured by volume. Plan on 2 ounces dry pasta per serving for a first course or a side dish, 3 to 4 ounces for a main course. The general rule is 1 pound of pasta per four main-course servings.

☐ Four ounces uncooked pasta (1 cup dry) will equal 2½ cups cooked elbow macaroni, shells, rotini, cavatelli, wheels, mostaccioli, penne, ziti.

☐ Four ounces uncooked or a 1-inch diameter bunch dry pasta will equal 2 cups cooked spaghetti, capellini (angel-hair), vermicelli, linguine.

Cooking Tips

☐ Boil pasta in a large deep pot. Use at least 4 quarts of water for each pound of pasta (1 quart for each 4 ounces). Bring it to a rapidly rolling boil before adding pasta for even cooking without sticking. Salt is not necessary for proper cooking, though it may be added for flavor. It is also not necessary to add oil to the cooking water.

☐ Add pasta to water all at once. Stir gently until water returns to a boil. If long strands of spaghetti don't fit in the pot, use a wooden spoon to bend them gently just below the water line. Do not cover pasta during cooking unless specifically directed in the recipe. Stir frequently with a wooden spoon or fork to keep strands separated.

☐ Cooking time varies from 5 to 20 minutes, depending on size, shape and degree of doneness or firmness desired, as well as brand. To avoid overcooking, use package directions as a guide but begin checking pasta a few minutes before the time stated on the package. Test for doneness by tasting; properly cooked pasta is tender but firm—*al dente* ("to the bite or tooth"). Or press a piece against the side of the pot with a fork; it will break easily and cleanly if done.

☐ Drain at once in a colander. Do not rinse unless recipe specifically says to do so. Shake colander to drain as much water as possible. Combine in a heated bowl with other ingredients or top with sauce and serve at once.

☐ Reduce pasta's boiling time by about one third when it is to be cooked further in a casserole.

☐ Pasta is at its best freshly cooked, but cooked pasta can be refrigerated up to one week. Toss it with a little oil to prevent sticking. To reheat, drop into boiling water briefly, drain and use immediately. Cooked pasta stored in sauce softens and loses texture.

Fresh Pasta

☐ Keep fresh pasta tightly covered in the refrigerator up to one week or in the freezer up to one month. You don't have to thaw before cooking.

☐ Unlike dry pasta, which doubles in volume when cooked, fresh pasta hardly swells at all.

☐ All fresh pasta is made with egg. Fresh pasta often comes in flavors and colors, from the common (spinach) to the exotic (green peppercorn). It may also be flavored with carrots, parsley, tomato, mushroom or lemon. Experiment to find your favorites.

☐ Because fresh pasta cooks so quickly, you should have the sauce prepared, a colander and serving dish ready and the table set before you put the pasta in the boiling water. Use plenty of water (1 quart for every 4 ounces) to keep pasta pieces moving and separate while they cook. Add all the pasta to the rapidly boiling water at once.

As you stir the pasta it will begin to soften and submerge. At that point, you may want to cover the pot briefly to help bring the water back to a rolling boil; then uncover and continue cooking.

☐ Package directions tend to overestimate cooking times. Only trust the *al dente* test and start tasting early!

Pasta Cheeses

There are three categories of cheeses most often used in pasta dishes: the hard grating cheeses like Parmesan and Romano, melting cheeses like mozzarella, Cheddar and Fontina, and the ricotta-type cheeses used for fillings. Below is a more detailed description of some pasta cheeses.

Parmesan

☐ Italians don't sprinkle grated Parmesan over every pasta dish, but when they do it's because they wish to add a delicate, mildly salty flavor to the pasta.

☐ Parmesan of different qualities is sold in many forms. Most familiar is pregrated Parmesan packed in jars or round cardboard containers. While it can't be beat for convenience, it lacks the flavor and body of freshly grated cheese. An alternative, which is just as easy to use, is the freshly grated cheese sold at many supermarket cheese counters and in cheese shops. The price is higher, but so is the quality.

☐ To bring out the best in your pasta dishes, we recommend purchasing Parmesan in wedges or chunks and grating just what you need. Chunks of cheese hold their flavor longer than grated cheese does. Domestically produced Parmesan is widely available at supermarket cheese counters.

☐ The most wonderful Parmesan of all is Parmesan Reggiano, known to Italians as the king of cheeses. It is produced only in certain provinces in Italy and aged for at least eighteen months, which gives the cheese its characteristic granular texture. If it is available in your area, do splurge on a chunk and grate it fresh over a favorite recipe. It is also a delicious table cheese, accompanied by crusty bread or ripe sweet pears.

☐ Parmesan is usually grated, but for some dishes and salads it is better to shred it. You can also use your food processor to grate Parmesan. Cut it in small chunks, removing any rind, and process in the work bowl with the steel blade. It won't really be "grated"; it will break up into tiny granular pieces.

☐ Grated or in a chunk, Parmesan must always be kept well wrapped and refrigerated.

Romano

☐ Italy's oldest known cheese has a spicy sharp flavor and is sold in pieces or grated. It can be substituted for Parmesan in many recipes, but it is not as mild. You can combine Parmesan and Romano to vary the flavor of favorite recipes.

Mozzarella

☐ A melting cheese with not much flavor, mozzarella is shredded or sliced and often used in baked dishes, such as lasagne, providing those long, delicious gooey strands.

☐ Mozzarella is sold in supermarkets, usually in 8-ounce pieces, and also comes in a lower-fat variety. For ease, buy it preshredded in bags.

☐ Fresh mozzarella is really special; happily, it is becoming much easier to find. It is quite perishable and usually sold packed in water or marinated in herbs, olive oil or crushed red pepper. Fresh mozzarella should not be baked for long periods of time or it will become watery. It is scrumptious cut in small pieces and tossed with hot pasta, or sliced and served with fresh ripe or dried tomatoes, basil and olive oil.

Ricotta

☐ A cousin to cottage cheese but with a sweeter, milder flavor, ricotta is generally used in fillings for lasagne or stuffed shells. It is sold in tubs and comes in a part-skim version.

Tomato Sauces

Angel-Hair Pasta with Dried Tomato and Basil Sauce

This recipe is equally good hot or cold.

12 ounces angel-hair pasta (capellini)
 3 tablespoons olive oil
 1 tablespoon butter or margarine
 2 teaspoons minced fresh garlic
 1 *each* large red and green bell
     pepper, roasted, peeled and cut in
     thin strips (see Roasting Peppers,
     page 9)
 1 cup loosely packed shredded fresh
     basil leaves
 3 tablespoons chopped fresh parsley
 2 tablespoons chopped dried tomatoes
     (see Dried Tomatoes, page 9)
 ½ teaspoon salt
 ¼ teaspoon pepper
Freshly grated Romano or Parmesan
     cheese (optional)

1. Bring a large pot of water to a boil over high heat. Add angel-hair pasta and cook according to package directions, stirring frequently, until firm to the bite. Drain in a colander.

2. Meanwhile, heat oil and butter in a large skillet over medium heat. Add garlic and cook 1 to 2 minutes, stirring occasionally, until soft and light golden.

3. Stir in bell peppers, basil, parsley, dried tomatoes, salt and pepper. Cook 1 to 2 minutes, stirring constantly, just until hot.

4. Transfer angel-hair pasta to a large heated serving bowl. Pour sauce over pasta and toss to coat. Serve immediately. Serve cheese on the side, if desired.

Makes 4 servings. Per serving: 456 calories, 12 grams protein, 70 grams carbohydrate, 14 grams fat, 8 milligrams cholesterol with butter, 0 milligrams cholesterol with margarine, 381 milligrams sodium

Angel-Hair Pasta with Dried Tomato and Basil Sauce

Whole-Wheat Pasta with Grilled-Tomato Sauce

A tomato-season favorite from Alice Waters of Chez Panisse in Berkeley, California. Serve as a side dish with grilled lamb or veal chops. Tagliarine is a very narrow noodle.

- **4** large ripe fresh tomatoes (about 3 pounds), halved crosswise and seeded
- **1** medium-size red onion, sliced in ¼-inch rounds (about 1 cup)
- **6** tablespoons virgin olive oil
- **¾** teaspoon salt
- **¼** teaspoon pepper
- **½** cup loosely packed fresh marjoram sprigs, preferably with flowers, or 2 tablespoons dried marjoram
- **8** ounces whole-wheat tagliarine or spaghetti
- **2** teaspoons minced fresh garlic

1. Prepare barbecue grill or turn on broiler.

2. Brush tomatoes and onion with 2 tablespoons of the oil and sprinkle with salt and pepper. Fill empty tomato-seed pockets with marjoram sprigs and flowers.

3. Grill tomatoes over medium-hot coals or broil 4 inches from heat source 8 to 10 minutes, turning tomatoes once and onion slices a few times, until tender and browned. Transfer to a cutting board. Roughly chop tomatoes and marjoram.

4. Meanwhile, bring a large pot of water to a boil over high heat. Add tagliarine and cook according to package directions, stirring frequently, until firm to the bite. Drain in a colander.

5. Heat remaining 4 tablespoons oil in a medium-size saucepan over medium heat. Add chopped tomatoes, onion and garlic. Simmer about 5 minutes to blend flavors.

6. Transfer pasta to a large heated serving bowl. Pour sauce over pasta. Toss to coat well and serve.

Makes 4 side-dish servings. Per serving: 437 calories, 10 grams protein, 55 grams carbohydrate, 22 grams fat, 0 milligrams cholesterol, 413 milligrams sodium

Spaghetti with Fresh Tomato Sauce

A simple and simply delicious dish that makes the most of ripe summer tomatoes.

    1 pound spaghetti
    ½ cup vegetable oil
    1 cup chopped onion
    3 small cloves garlic, minced
    6 large ripe fresh tomatoes, peeled
         (see Peeling Tomatoes, below),
         and coarsely chopped
    ⅓ cup chopped fresh parsley
    2 tablespoons chopped fresh
         basil leaves or 1½ teaspoons
         dried basil
    1½ teaspoons salt
    ½ teaspoon pepper

1. Bring a large pot of water to a boil over high heat. Add spaghetti and cook according to package directions, stirring frequently, until firm to the bite. Drain in a colander.

2. Meanwhile, heat oil in a large skillet over medium heat. Add onion and garlic and cook, stirring occasionally, until tender.

3. Stir tomatoes, parsley, basil, salt and pepper into skillet. Bring to a simmer and cook 10 minutes, stirring occasionally, until slightly thickened.

4. Transfer spaghetti to a large heated serving bowl. Pour sauce over spaghetti and toss lightly. Serve immediately.

Makes 4 servings. Per serving: 743 calories, 18 grams protein, 103 grams carbohydrate, 29 grams fat, 0 milligrams cholesterol, 817 milligrams sodium

---

Peeling Tomatoes

☐ Bring a medium-size saucepan of water to a boil over high heat. One or two at a time, plunge tomatoes into boiling water and boil 20 to 30 seconds, until the skin starts to feel loose. (The firmer the tomato, the longer the boiling time.) Lift from water with a slotted spoon and rinse briefly under cold running water. Slip off skins.

☐ If you have a gas stove, you can loosen the skins directly over the flames. Poke a long-handled meat fork through the tomato to hold it and turn over the flame until the skin changes color slightly and bursts in one or two places. Let sit until cool and peel off skin. This method adds a wonderful, slightly charred flavor to the tomatoes and is perfect for Mexican- or Southwest-inspired recipes.

From the Garden

🕐 **MAKE-AHEAD**
★ **SPECIAL—AND WORTH IT**

Confetti Pasta

(Shown on page 4)

From Anthony Bourdain, a chef in New York City, comes this new version of pasta primavera. You can make the carrot butter and blanch the other vegetables a day ahead (see Blanching Vegetables, page 11), or blanch them in the boiling water just before adding the pasta.

    1 small carrot, diced and blanched
         (about ⅓ cup)
    2 medium-size cloves garlic
    ½ cup unsalted butter
    12 ounces rotelle or rotini
    ½ cup dry white wine
    1 tablespoon chopped shallot or onion
    1 tablespoon olive oil
    2 cups small broccoli florets,
         blanched (buy a 1¼-pound bunch,
         save stems for another use)
    8 ounces snow-peas, trimmed, cut in
         strips and blanched (about 3 cups)
    8 ounces yellow summer squash, cut in narrow
         strips and blanched (about 1 cup)
    ¼ cup chopped pistachio nuts (optional)

1. Put carrot and garlic in a food processor or a blender and process until finely chopped. Add butter and process until blended. Scrape into a small bowl and cover and refrigerate until firm.

2. Bring a large pot of water to a boil over high heat. Add pasta and cook according to package directions, stirring frequently, until firm to the bite. Drain in a colander.

3. Meanwhile, boil wine and shallot in a small heavy skillet over high heat until only about 1 tablespoon liquid is left. Reduce heat to low and whisk in carrot butter 1 tablespoon at a time until mixture is creamy. (Sauce separates if cooked over higher heat.) Remove from heat and cover to keep warm.

4. Heat oil in a large skillet over medium-high heat. Add blanched vegetables and toss 1 to 2 minutes, until heated.

5. Transfer pasta to a large heated serving bowl. Pour in sauce and vegetables and toss to coat well. Sprinkle nuts on top, if desired, and serve.

Makes 6 servings. Per serving (without pistachio nuts): 433 calories, 11 grams protein, 52 grams carbohydrate, 21 grams fat, 40 milligrams cholesterol, 19 milligrams sodium

Rotelle with Vegetables and Parmesan Sauce

1 tablespoon olive or vegetable oil
1 bag (16 ounces) frozen mixed
    broccoli, carrots and cauliflower
1 box (10 ounces) frozen lima beans
1 medium-size onion, sliced in thin
    rounds (about 1 cup)
1 jar (about 32 ounces) plain
    spaghetti sauce
1 pound rotelle
⅓ cup grated Parmesan cheese

1. Heat oil in a Dutch oven over medium-high heat. Add frozen mixed vegetables, lima beans and onion. Cover and cook 8 to 10 minutes, stirring twice, until vegetables are crisp-tender.

2. Stir in spaghetti sauce and bring to a boil. Reduce heat to medium-low. Cover and simmer 8 to 10 minutes, stirring twice, until vegetables are tender. Remove from heat.

3. Meanwhile, bring a large pot of water to a boil over high heat. Add rotelle and cook according to package directions, stirring frequently, until firm to the bite. Drain in a colander. Transfer to a large heated serving bowl.

4. Sprinkle cheese over sauce and stir gently to mix. Spoon sauce over pasta; toss and serve.

Makes 4 servings, 5½ cups sauce. Per serving: 781 calories, 29 grams protein, 137 grams carbohydrate, 12 grams fat, 8 milligrams cholesterol, 1,741 milligrams sodium

---

Blanching Vegetables

☐ Bring a medium-size or large pot of water to a boil over high heat. (Size of pot depends on the volume of vegetables. They need to float freely in the water, and you want the water to return to a boil quickly.) Salt water if blanching green vegetables to bring out the color. Have a bowl of ice water ready.

☐ Add vegetables to boiling water and cook just until crisp-tender and brightly colored. Remove immediately with a strainer and plunge into ice water. Cool completely and drain well.

♥ LOW-CALORIE

Pasta with Vegetables and Herb Sauce

To keep the calorie count down, this dish uses low-fat milk, low-fat ricotta cheese and plenty of vegetables.

Herb Sauce
¼ cup 2%-fat milk
¼ cup low-fat ricotta cheese
¼ cup grated Parmesan cheese
½ cup packed fresh parsley leaves
2 medium-size green onions, cut up
10 fresh basil leaves or 2 teaspoons
    dried basil
1 small clove garlic, cut up

Pasta and Vegetables
4 ounces fettuccine
4 medium-size carrots, cut in
    ¼-inch-thick rounds (about
    2½ cups)
1 cup small broccoli florets
1¼ cups coarsely shredded yellow
    summer squash
1 medium-size zucchini (about 7
    ounces), quartered lengthwise,
    then sliced ¼-inch-thick
    crosswise
½ cup snow-peas (about 2 ounces),
    ends trimmed

1. Put milk, ricotta, Parmesan, parsley, green onions, basil and garlic in a food processor or blender. Process until puréed.

2. Bring a large pot of water to a boil over high heat. Stir in fettuccine and carrots and boil 6 minutes, stirring frequently. Stir in broccoli and boil 2 minutes. Stir in squashes and boil 1 to 2 minutes, until pasta is firm to the bite and vegetables are crisp-tender. Just before draining, stir in snow-peas. Drain vegetables and pasta in a colander. Shake to remove excess water.

3. Transfer pasta and vegetables to a large heated serving bowl. Pour in sauce. Toss to coat well and serve immediately.

Makes 4 servings. Per serving: 237 calories, 12 grams protein, 38 grams carbohydrate, 5 grams fat, 39 milligrams cholesterol, 121 milligrams sodium

Pasta Primavera

Pasta Primavera

8 ounces medium-size pasta shells
1 can (19 ounces) chick-peas, rinsed
and drained
1 package (16 ounces) frozen mixed
broccoli, cauliflower and
red peppers
1 jar (about 15½ ounces)
spaghetti sauce
⅓ cup water
¼ cup grated Parmesan cheese

1. Bring a large pot of water to a boil over high heat. Add pasta shells and cook according to package directions, stirring frequently, until firm to the bite. Drain in a colander.

2. Meanwhile, put chick-peas, vegetables, spaghetti sauce and water in a large heavy skillet. Bring to a boil over high heat. Reduce heat to medium-low. Cover and simmer 10 minutes, until vegetables are tender. Remove from heat and stir in cheese.

3. Transfer pasta shells to a large heated serving bowl. Spoon sauce over pasta; toss well and serve.

Makes 4 servings. Per serving: 454 calories, 19 grams protein, 74 grams carbohydrate, 8 grams fat, 6 milligrams cholesterol, 826 milligrams sodium

Prepared Sauces

Many of our recipes call for pre-made sauces which are a really wonderful convenience food, great to have in the pantry for a quick dinner. Prepared sauces come in jars or cans on grocery shelves or in tubs refrigerated in the dairy case. Experiment with different flavors and brands to find your favorites. Concerned about calories? Check the labels. The nutrition information for our recipes is based on an average of several brands.

Pasta with Creamy Vegetable Sauce

The secret of this recipe is the cream cheese, which makes the texture silky-smooth.

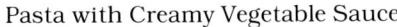

12 ounces fettuccine
 3 tablespoons butter or margarine
 1 cup thinly sliced mushrooms
 1 package (10 ounces) frozen broccoli
      florets, thawed and drained, or 2
      cups fresh, cooked crisp-tender
 1 tub container (8 ounces) soft cream
      cheese with toasted onion
 ¾ cup half-and-half or milk
 ¾ teaspoon salt
 ½ teaspoon pepper

1. Bring a large pot of water to a boil over high heat. Add fettuccine and cook according to package directions, stirring frequently, until firm to the bite. Drain in a colander.

2. Meanwhile, melt butter in a large pot or Dutch oven over medium heat. Add mushrooms and cook about 5 minutes, stirring frequently, until tender.

3. Add broccoli and cook 1 minute, stirring constantly. Add cream cheese and cook, stirring constantly with a wooden spoon, until completely melted.

4. Reduce heat to low and stir in half-and-half, salt and pepper. Simmer 3 minutes, stirring constantly, until hot. Add fettuccine to sauce and toss to coat. Cook just until hot. Transfer to a large heated serving bowl. Serve immediately.

Makes 4 servings. Per serving (with half-and-half): 673 calories, 19 grams protein, 72 grams carbohydrate, 34 grams fat, 128 milligrams cholesterol with butter, 101 milligrams cholesterol with margarine, 813 milligrams sodium

Pasta with Creamy Vegetable Sauce

Spaghetti with Spring Vegetables

The asparagus in this dish tells you spring is here.

      3 tablespoons vegetable oil
      1 tablespoon dried basil leaves
      1 teaspoon minced fresh garlic
      1 pound asparagus, tough ends snapped off,
          cut in ½-inch diagonal slices
      2 large fresh tomatoes, chopped
      1 medium-size zucchini, sliced
          ¼-inch thick
      2 green onions, cut in ½-inch lengths
      8 ounces spaghetti
      8 ounces mushrooms, sliced (about 4 cups)
      ½ cup chicken broth
      1 teaspoon salt
      2 tablespoons grated Parmesan cheese

1. Heat oil in a large skillet over medium-high heat. Add basil and garlic and stir a few seconds. Add asparagus, tomatoes, zucchini and green onions. Cook 8 to 10 minutes, stirring frequently, until asparagus is almost crisp-tender.

2. Meanwhile, bring a large pot of water to a boil over high heat. Add spaghetti and cook according to package directions, stirring frequently, until firm to the bite. Drain in a colander.

3. Add mushrooms, broth and salt to asparagus mixture. Cook 5 minutes, stirring occasionally, until asparagus is crisp-tender. Reduce heat to low and add hot spaghetti and Parmesan. Toss well to mix and cook just until hot. Transfer to a heated serving platter. Serve immediately.

Makes 4 servings. Per serving: 389 calories, 14 grams protein, 59 grams carbohydrate, 12 grams fat, 4 milligrams cholesterol, 658 milligrams sodium

Chopping Garlic

☐ Purchase the freshest garlic available. Heads should be firm with no musty smell. Avoid garlic that has little green shoots at the ends of cloves.

☐ To peel garlic, lay a clove flat on a cutting board and crush lightly with the flat side of a heavy knife to break and loosen skin. Remove papery skin. Slice off the little brown end of the clove and mince the clove with the knife. For easy measuring, scrape minced garlic from the board with the knife and scrape it off the knife with a smaller knife or flexible metal spatula.

☐ Rub a cut lemon on your hands and on cutting board to remove garlic smell. It's a good idea to save one cutting board just for garlic and onions.

Pasta Cooking Tools

☐ **Cooking Pot:** Every kitchen needs at least one large pot of a minimum 6-quart capacity for cooking pasta. It can be of any material you like, but stainless steel is preferable because it lasts the longest and won't pit, as aluminum does. A lid for the pot is helpful; a covered pot of water comes to a boil faster.

☐ **Colander:** The easiest way to drain pasta is to pour it into a colander set in the sink. You'll need one with plenty of holes so the water drains out quickly. Shake colander to remove excess water.

☐ **Wooden Spoon or Fork:** A long-handled spoon or fork will make it easy to stir pasta as it cooks, keeping your sleeves out of the hot water.

☐ **Grater:** Very hard cheeses such as Parmesan are generally grated finely on the small holes of a grater. Softer cheeses such as mozzarella and Cheddar are shredded on the larger holes. The most useful grater has four sides with a variety of hole sizes for all uses and a slicing blade for making fine shreds of zucchini or cucumber.

Fettuccine with Vegetables

Fettuccine with Vegetables

To save time, buy the Monterey Jack cheese already shredded in an 8-ounce bag.

- 1 **tablespoon salt**
- 1 **package (9 ounces) frozen Italian green beans**
- 1 **package (about 9 ounces) fresh fettuccine**
- 2 **medium-size yellow summer squash (about 8 ounces each), sliced in thin rounds**
- 3 **tablespoons butter or margarine**
- 2 **tablespoons all-purpose flour**
- 1½ **cups milk**
- 2 **cups shredded Monterey Jack cheese (8 ounces)**
- ¼ **cup grated Parmesan cheese**
- 1 **tablespoon thinly sliced fresh basil leaves or 1 teaspoon dried basil**
- ¼ **teaspoon crushed red-pepper flakes (optional)**

1. Bring a large pot of water and the salt to a boil over high heat. Add beans and cook 3 minutes. Stir in fettuccine and squash. Return to a boil and boil 2 minutes longer, until vegetables are crisp-tender and pasta is firm to the bite. Drain in a colander.

2. Return pasta and vegetables to cooking pot and toss with 1 tablespoon of the butter to prevent sticking.

3. Meanwhile, melt remaining 2 tablespoons butter in a medium-size saucepan over medium heat. Reduce heat to low. Add flour and cook about 1 minute, stirring constantly, until smooth and frothy. Gradually stir in milk.

4. Raise heat under saucepan to medium and cook until sauce boils and thickens, stirring frequently. Reduce heat to low and add cheeses, basil and crushed red pepper, if desired. Stir just until cheese melts.

5. Transfer fettuccine and vegetables to a large heated serving bowl. Pour sauce over pasta; toss to coat and serve immediately.

Makes 4 servings. Per serving: 612 calories, 30 grams protein, 52 grams carbohydrate, 33 grams fat, 207 milligrams cholesterol with butter, 180 milligrams cholesterol with margarine, 552 milligrams sodium

Zucchini Ziti

To remove the seeds from peeled tomatoes, core tomatoes and cut in quarters. Scrape out seeds with your fingers or a teaspoon.

- **2 tablespoons butter or margarine**
- **½ cup chopped onion**
- **4 large ripe fresh tomatoes (1½ pounds), peeled (see Peeling Tomatoes, page 10), seeded and chopped, or 2 cans (14½ ounces each), drained and chopped (about 4 cups)**
- **1½ pounds zucchini, sliced ⅛ inch thick (about 6 cups)**
- **1 green bell pepper, coarsely chopped (about 1 cup)**
- **¾ teaspoon salt**
- **½ teaspoon dried basil leaves**
- **¼ teaspoon dried oregano leaves**
- **¼ teaspoon dried thyme leaves**
- **1 can (4 ounces) mushroom pieces, drained**
- **8 ounces ziti or rigatoni**
- **Grated Parmesan cheese (optional)**

1. Melt butter in a large skillet over medium-high heat. Add onion and cook 2 minutes. Add tomatoes, zucchini, bell pepper, salt, basil, oregano and thyme. Reduce heat to low. Cover and cook 20 minutes, stirring occasionally, until zucchini is tender.

2. Add mushrooms and cook 3 minutes longer, until tender.

3. Meanwhile, bring a large pot of water to a boil. Add ziti and cook according to package directions, stirring frequently, until firm to the bite. Drain in a colander. Transfer to a large heated serving bowl.

4. Pour sauce over ziti. Sprinkle with Parmesan cheese, if desired, and serve.

Makes 4 servings. Per serving (without Parmesan): 351 calories, 12 grams protein, 61 grams carbohydrate, 7 grams fat, 18 milligrams cholesterol with butter, 0 milligrams cholesterol with margarine, 485 milligrams sodium

Spaghetti with Zucchini, Corn and Mozzarella

A fresh-tasting meatless sauce, gooey with strands of melted mozzarella cheese. Use fresh mozzarella if it's available in your market. Serve with crusty bread.

- **1 pound spaghetti**
- **1 tablespoon olive or vegetable oil**
- **3 small zucchini (12 ounces), quartered lengthwise and cut in ¼-inch pieces (about 2 cups)**
- **1 jar (about 32 ounces) plain spaghetti sauce**
- **1 can (8¾ ounces) corn kernels, drained**
- **1 cup shredded part-skim mozzarella cheese (4 ounces)**

1. Bring a large pot of water to a boil over high heat. Add spaghetti and cook according to package directions, stirring frequently, until firm to the bite. Drain in a colander.

2. Meanwhile, heat oil in a Dutch oven over medium-high heat. Add zucchini and cook 3 to 5 minutes, stirring frequently, until it begins to brown and is almost tender.

3. Stir in spaghetti sauce and corn and bring to a boil. Reduce heat to medium-low, cover and simmer 6 to 8 minutes, stirring twice, until zucchini is tender. Remove from heat.

4. Transfer spaghetti to a large heated serving bowl. Pour sauce over pasta and sprinkle with cheese. Toss just until cheese melts and serve immediately.

Makes 4 servings, 5 cups sauce. Per serving: 768 calories, 29 grams protein, 127 grams carbohydrate, 15 grams fat, 15 milligrams cholesterol, 1,781 milligrams sodium

Spaghetti with Zucchini-Tomato Sauce

For a change of pace, use fusilli pasta instead of spaghetti.

- 1 tablespoon vegetable oil
- 1 large onion, chopped (about 1 cup)
- 1 large clove garlic, minced
- 1 can (28 ounces) Italian-style tomatoes, broken up
- ¾ teaspoon dried oregano, crumbled, or to taste
- ½ teaspoon salt, or to taste
- ¼ teaspoon granulated sugar
- ¼ teaspoon pepper
- 4 small zucchini (about 1¼ pounds), cut in 2 × ½-inch sticks
- 1 pound spaghetti

1. Heat oil in a large saucepan over medium heat. Add onion and garlic and cook until tender and golden, stirring occasionally.

2. Stir tomatoes, oregano, salt, sugar and pepper into saucepan and bring to a boil. Reduce heat to medium-low and simmer sauce until slightly thickened, stirring occasionally.

3. Stir in zucchini. Cover and simmer about 10 minutes, until zucchini is tender.

4. Meanwhile, bring a large pot of water to a boil over high heat. Add spaghetti and cook according to package directions, stirring frequently, until firm to the bite. Drain in a colander. Transfer to a large heated serving bowl and pour sauce over spaghetti. Toss and serve.

Makes 4 servings. Per serving: 525 calories, 17 grams protein, 103 grams carbohydrate, 5 grams fat, 0 milligrams cholesterol, 534 milligrams sodium

Linguine with Orange Sauce

This unusual dish makes a refreshing appetizer for four or a main course for two.

- ¼ cup finely chopped shallots or green onions
- ¾ cup dry white wine or ¼ cup fresh-squeezed orange juice
- 9 ounces fresh or 6 ounces dry linguine
- 1 cup heavy cream
- ⅔ cup grated Parmesan cheese
- 1½ teaspoons grated fresh orange peel

1. Bring shallots and wine to a boil in a medium-size saucepan over medium-high heat. Boil until liquid is reduced to 1 tablespoon (8 to 9 minutes for wine, 3 to 4 minutes for orange juice).

2. Meanwhile, bring a large pot of water to a boil over high heat. Add linguine and cook according to package directions, stirring frequently, until firm to the bite. Drain in a colander.

3. Add cream to skillet and bring to a boil. Reduce heat to medium and cook about 4 minutes, until slightly thickened. Stir in cheese until smooth, then stir in orange peel and remove from heat.

4. Transfer linguine to a medium-size heated serving bowl. Pour sauce over pasta; toss to coat and serve.

Makes 2 main-dish or 4 appetizer servings. Per main-dish serving (with fresh pasta): 1,055 calories, 31 grams protein, 99 grams carbohydrate, 59 grams fat, 307 milligrams cholesterol, 289 milligrams sodium

Pasta with Ricotta, Spinach and Cream

There are only five ingredients in this soothing dish.

- 8 ounces penne or ziti
- 2 cups heavy cream
- ¾ cup ricotta cheese
- ¼ cup cooked spinach, squeezed dry and chopped (use freshly cooked or thawed frozen chopped spinach)
- Grated Parmesan cheese (optional)

1. Bring a large pot of water to a boil over high heat. Add penne and cook according to package directions, stirring frequently, until nearly tender (pasta should be slightly undercooked). Drain in a colander.

2. Pour cream into pasta cooking pot. Stir in ricotta and spinach and bring to a boil over medium heat, stirring frequently.

3. Stir in drained penne and continue cooking until sauce is slightly thickened and pasta is firm to the bite.

4. Spoon into bowls and sprinkle each serving with Parmesan, if desired. Serve immediately.

Makes 4 servings. Per serving (without Parmesan): 713 calories, 15 grams protein, 48 grams carbohydrate, 52 grams fat, 182 milligrams cholesterol, 111 milligrams sodium

Red, White and Green Capellini

Put spinach in refrigerator the night before to defrost. Pass grated Parmesan cheese at the table. On the side: tender leaves of Boston lettuce with a mild garlic dressing. Cannellini beans are generally found in the Italian-food section of supermarkets.

2 cups vegetable broth (see Note)
6 ounces capellini (angel-hair pasta),
    broken in thirds
1 teaspoon Worcestershire sauce
1 can (about 19 ounces) white beans,
    such as cannellini beans, drained
1 package (10 ounces) frozen chopped
    spinach, thawed, drained and
    squeezed dry
1 jar (4 ounces) pimientos, well drained
    and cut in thin strips

1. Put broth, capellini and Worcestershire sauce in a large skillet. Bring to a boil over high heat. Cover and boil 3 minutes, stirring three times with a fork to separate pasta strands.

2. Mix beans, spinach and pimientos in a small bowl. Spoon bean mixture over pasta. Cover and reduce heat to low. Simmer 3 to 4 minutes, until mixture is heated through and pasta is firm to the bite. Toss to mix.

3. Transfer to a medium-size heated serving bowl and serve immediately.

Makes 4 servings. Per serving: 314 calories, 16 grams protein, 60 grams carbohydrate, 2 grams fat, 2 milligrams cholesterol, 546 milligrams sodium

Note: You can use vegetarian-style bouillon cubes or instant broth granules to make the broth.

Red, White and Green Capellini

PESTO

Classic pesto is made with fresh basil, pignoli, olive oil and Parmesan cheese but as you will see, this sauce takes well to variation.

🕐 **MAKE-AHEAD**

Pesto

This classic sauce was considered exotic just a few years ago. Now it is available in jars, in plastic containers in the dairy case or frozen. Pesto is served over pasta at most Italian restaurants. The food processor makes it easy to make your own pesto from fragrant fresh basil. When basil is abundant, make several batches of pesto (omitting the cheese; stir it in just before serving or using) and freeze in airtight containers with a little olive oil drizzled over the surface. The frozen sauce may darken, but the flavor will still be delicious. This recipe yields 1 cup, enough for 1 pound freshly cooked pasta.

> 2 cups loosely packed fresh
>   basil leaves
> 2 cloves garlic, crushed
> ¼ cup walnuts or pignoli (pine nuts,
>   see Pignoli, page 21)
> ½ to ¾ cup olive oil
> ½ cup freshly grated Parmesan cheese
> Salt to taste

1. Process basil, garlic, walnuts and ½ cup oil in a food processor or blender until almost smooth. (If sauce is pasty, add additional oil.)

2. Scrape into a small bowl and beat in cheese and salt. Taste and add more salt, if desired. Refrigerate up to five days or freeze until ready to use.

Makes about 1 cup. Per 2 tablespoons (with walnuts and ½ cup oil): 165 calories, 3 grams protein, 1 gram carbohydrate, 17 grams fat, 5 milligrams cholesterol, 111 milligrams sodium

Pasta with Pesto Cream

> 12 ounces fettuccine
> ¼ cup walnuts, coarsely chopped
> ¼ cup chopped green onions
> 1 tablespoon olive oil
> 1½ cups chopped fresh tomatoes
> ½ cup pesto (homemade or bought;
>   see Pesto recipe, this page)
> ½ cup heavy cream
> 2 tablespoons grated
>   Parmesan cheese

1. Bring a large pot of water to a boil over high heat. Add fettuccine and cook according to package directions, stirring frequently, until firm to the bite. Drain in a colander.

2. Meanwhile, heat a medium-size skillet over medium heat. Add walnuts and cook 2 to 3 minutes, shaking often, until lightly toasted.

3. Stir in green onions and oil. When onions are wilted, add tomatoes and cook 2 to 3 minutes, until tender. Stir in pesto and cream and bring to a boil.

4. Transfer pasta to a large heated serving bowl; pour in sauce and toss well. Sprinkle cheese over pasta and serve.

Makes 4 servings. Per serving: 838 calories, 20 grams protein, 76 grams carbohydrate, 51 grams fat, 42 milligrams cholesterol, 542 milligrams sodium

---

Basil

This beautiful aromatic herb is the basis for most pesto sauces and adds zest to pasta recipes. Buy basil fresh in a big bunch or grow it in your garden or in a pot on the windowsill. Store basil unwashed. Stand the stems in a jar of water, cover the leaves with a plastic bag and refrigerate, changing water every two days. Basil will keep fresh for three to five days. Wash well before using. Generally just the leaves are used in a pesto or other puréed sauce, but small, tender stems can be used, too.

Pasta with Parsley Pesto

This recipe was developed for *Woman's Day* by the great James Beard, who was a frequent contributor.

- 1 pound fettuccine or medium-size egg noodles
- 2 large bunches parsley, coarse stems broken off (about 4 cups)
- 1 cup walnuts
- ¾ cup small chunks Parmesan cheese
- 1 cup olive oil
- 3 large cloves garlic
- ½ teaspoon salt, or to taste
- ¼ cup butter or margarine
- 1 pint basket (about 2½ cups) cherry tomatoes
- ¼ cup minced fresh dill

1. Bring a large pot of water to a boil over high heat. Add fettuccine and cook according to package directions, stirring frequently, until firm to the bite. Drain in a colander.

2. Meanwhile, put parsley, walnuts, Parmesan, oil, garlic and salt in a food processor and process until nearly smooth.

3. Melt butter in a large skillet over very low heat. Add tomatoes and dill. Cook, shaking pan occasionally, until tomatoes are well glazed and heated through (do not cook until they burst).

4. Arrange fettuccine on a heated platter. Spoon pesto over fettuccine and arrange tomatoes around the edge. Toss pasta lightly with pesto and serve.

Makes 4 generous servings. Per serving: 1,287 calories, 27 grams protein, 96 grams carbohydrate, 91 grams fat, 159 milligrams cholesterol with butter, 123 milligrams cholesterol with margarine, 554 milligrams sodium

Spaghetti with Spinach Pesto

Another delicious variation of pesto. Look for the smooth, large-leaved spinach, sometimes called New Zealand spinach. It is easier to wash than the crinkly-type spinach.

- 1 pound spaghetti
- ⅓ cup walnuts
- ⅓ cup water
- 2 large cloves garlic, cut up
- 2 cups packed spinach leaves, rinsed and well drained
- ½ cup olive oil
- ¼ cup grated Parmesan cheese
- 1 teaspoon salt

1. Bring a large pot of water to a boil over high heat. Add spaghetti and cook according to package directions, stirring frequently, until firm to the bite. Drain in a colander.

2. Meanwhile, put walnuts, water and garlic in a food processor or a blender. Process until finely chopped. Gradually add spinach alternately with oil and process until smooth. Add Parmesan and salt and process until blended.

3. Transfer spaghetti to a large heated serving bowl. Pour pesto over pasta and toss well. Serve immediately.

Makes 4 servings. Per serving: 761 calories, 19 grams protein, 89 grams carbohydrate, 37 grams fat, 5 milligrams cholesterol, 699 milligrams sodium

⏱ **MAKE-AHEAD**
♥ **LOW-CALORIE**

Cottage-Cheese Pesto

Serve this low-calorie version of the classic fresh-herb sauce over spaghetti or spinach linguine.

- ¼ cup walnuts or pignoli (pine nuts, see Pignoli, page 21)
- 3 cloves garlic, halved
- 1 cup low-fat cottage cheese
- 4 cups loosely packed torn fresh basil leaves
- ½ cup packed fresh parsley, thick stems removed
- 1 green onion, cut up
- ½ teaspoon salt
- ¼ teaspoon pepper

1. Put walnuts and garlic in a food processor and process until finely chopped. Add remaining ingredients in order listed; whirl until basil and parsley are finely chopped, scraping down sides of bowl as needed.

2. Transfer to a small bowl or jar with a tight-fitting cover. Place plastic wrap directly on surface; cover tightly. Refrigerate up to two days. Stir before using, as surface may discolor.

Makes 4 servings, 1½ cups, enough for 1 pound cooked pasta. Per serving (with walnuts): 87 calories, 9 grams protein, 4 grams carbohydrate, 5 grams fat, 2 milligrams cholesterol, 266 milligrams sodium

Linguine with Italian Walnut Sauce

You can keep this flavorful no-cook sauce in the refrigerator up to two days—just bring it to room temperature before tossing with hot linguine. The recipe makes a perfect first course followed by grilled lamb chops. Or serve it as a main course for two with a big fruit salad for dessert.

    9 ounces fresh or 6 ounces
        dry linguine
    1 cup walnuts
    1 teaspoon minced fresh garlic
    2 tablespoons fresh-squeezed
        lemon juice
  ¼ cup chopped fresh parsley
  ¾ cup (6 ounces) ricotta cheese
  ½ cup milk
  ½ teaspoon salt, or to taste
  ⅛ teaspoon pepper, or to taste
  ¼ cup olive oil

1. Bring a large pot of water to a boil over high heat. Add linguine and cook according to package directions, stirring frequently, until firm to the bite. Drain in a colander.

2. Put walnuts, garlic and lemon juice in a food processor or blender and process until walnuts and garlic are finely chopped. Turn off motor. Add remaining ingredients except oil in order listed. Process just until mixture is blended and flecked with green. Add oil all at once and process just to mix.

3. Transfer pasta to a medium-size heated serving bowl; add sauce and toss to mix well. Serve immediately.

Makes 2 main-dish or 4 appetizer servings. Per main-dish serving (with fresh pasta): 1,265 calories, 36 grams protein, 106 grams carbohydrate, 79 grams fat, 251 milligrams cholesterol, 652 milligrams sodium

Mediterranean Pasta Sauce

A colorful change of pace from traditional pasta sauces and very Italian. To serve, heat sauce and toss with freshly cooked pasta shells or wheels.

  ½ cup olive oil
  ½ cup vegetable oil
    1 cup chopped fresh parsley
  ¾ cup Greek-style black olives, pitted
        and halved
  ¾ cup roasted red peppers (from a jar),
        cut in large pieces
  ½ cup pignoli (pine nuts, see Pignoli,
        below)
    2 cloves garlic, minced
  ¾ teaspoon salt, or to taste

1. Stir all ingredients in a medium-size bowl until well blended.

2. Toss with freshly cooked pasta and serve. Or spoon into a 2½-cup glass container, float a little more oil on top to cover completely, seal tightly and store in the refrigerator up to one week.

Makes 2½ cups, enough for 1 pound cooked pasta.
Per serving of sauce: 720 calories, 7 grams protein, 9 grams carbohydrate, 77 grams fat, 0 milligrams cholesterol, 1,790 milligrams sodium

---

Pignoli

☐ Pignoli, or pine nuts, are the kernels inside the cones of certain varieties of pine trees. They can be bought in supermarkets in small jars from the spice shelves (an expensive way to go) or in larger quantities at a much better price in supermarket health-food sections or stores.

☐ Use pignoli raw or toast them to bring out their flavor, but be sure to taste them before using to assure freshness. To toast pignoli, shake in a small dry skillet over medium-high heat until lightly browned. Tip out of skillet immediately onto a plate so that they don't continue cooking. You may also toast pignoli in a microwave oven.

Pasta with Beans

Pasta with Swiss Chard and Lentils

This recipe comes from Annie Somerville, director of the Greens restaurant in San Francisco. It is good with crusty Italian bread, and sliced oranges for dessert.

1 cup dried lentils, picked over, rinsed
    and drained
2 cups water
Two 1½-inch-long bay leaves
¾ teaspoon salt
2 teaspoons minced fresh garlic
1 teaspoon dried thyme leaves
1 teaspoon dried oregano leaves
8 ounces linguine
1 pound Swiss chard, rinsed, stems cut
    in ½-inch lengths; leaves stacked
    and cut crosswise in ½-inch-wide
    strips
¼ cup fresh-squeezed lemon juice
¼ cup finely chopped fresh parsley
2 tablespoons olive oil
¼ teaspoon pepper
1 cup grated Parmesan cheese

1. Put lentils, water, bay leaves and ½ teaspoon of the salt in a medium-size saucepan. Bring to a boil over high heat. Reduce heat to low. Cover and simmer 25 minutes, stirring occasionally, until lentils are tender. Discard bay leaves. Drain off water, stir in garlic, thyme and oregano and cover.

2. Bring a large pot of water to a boil over high heat. Add linguine and boil 4 minutes, stirring frequently. Stir in Swiss-chard stems and boil 2 minutes. Stir in Swiss-chard leaves and boil 2 minutes longer, until linguine is firm to the bite and stems are crisp-tender. Drain pasta and Swiss chard in a colander, reserving ¼ cup cooking water. Transfer to a large heated serving bowl.

3. Add lentils, reserved pasta water, lemon juice, parsley, oil, remaining ¼ teaspoon salt and the pepper to linguine and Swiss chard. Mix well. Sprinkle with Parmesan and serve.

Makes 4 servings. Per serving: 573 calories, 31 grams protein, 77 grams carbohydrate, 17 grams fat, 77 milligrams cholesterol, 769 milligrams sodium

---

Odds and Ends

☐ Is your pantry cluttered with a bit of this and a quarter package of that shape of pasta? Why not mix them! Mixing shapes and sizes is fun (and makes good sense). Just be sure the sizes are similar so they all cook in the same length of time. Otherwise start the larger ones first, adding the smaller pasta toward the end of cooking time.

☐ Left with half a can of tomato paste? Try this handy tip to save the remainder: Line a baking sheet with foil. Measure level tablespoons of tomato paste and drop on the foil, leaving space between each as if you were making cookies. Freeze until hard, then peel paste off foil. Store in a plastic freezer bag to add, frozen, to recipes.

What's in a Name?

The Italians whimsically named many pasta shapes and sizes after everyday things: cannelloni means "big pipes"; linguine, "small tongues"; manicotti, "little muffs"; mostaccioli, "small mustaches"; penne, "quills"; tubetti, "tubes"; and vermicelli, "little worms".

Mexican Spaghetti Pie

Use leftover spaghetti for this dish, or cook fresh. (To get 2 cups cooked spaghetti, cook 4 ounces dry.)

3 tablespoons vegetable oil
2 cups cooked spaghetti, cut up
½ cup chopped onion
1 cup diced fresh tomato
2 teaspoons chopped hot pickled peppers or ⅛ teaspoon crushed red-pepper flakes
1 can (15¼ to 16 ounces) red kidney beans, drained
3 large eggs
½ cup half-and-half or evaporated milk
¼ teaspoon salt
Pepper to taste
½ cup shredded Monterey Jack cheese

1. Heat oil in a 10-inch nonstick skillet over medium heat. Add spaghetti and onion and cook, stirring constantly, until onion is wilted and spaghetti is golden.

2. Add tomato and hot peppers and cook 2 minutes, stirring frequently, until hot. Press spaghetti lightly and evenly in bottom of skillet and sprinkle with beans.

3. Beat eggs, half-and-half, salt and pepper in a small bowl and pour over spaghetti. Sprinkle cheese over top. Cook about 4 minutes, until edges and bottom are set.

4. Cover, reduce heat to low and cook about 5 minutes, until cheese melts and eggs are set but slightly runny on top.

5. Broil 4 inches from heat source 2 minutes to firm the top. Cut in wedges and serve.

Makes 4 servings. Per serving (with half-and-half): 441 calories, 18 grams protein, 40 grams carbohydrate, 23 grams fat, 171 milligrams cholesterol, 275 milligrams sodium

Rotelle with Chick-pea, Carrot and Olive Sauce

Serve with dark pumpernickel and a wedge of Parmesan or Cheddar cheese.

1 pound rotelle
1 tablespoon olive or vegetable oil
2 medium-size carrots, scrubbed and very thinly sliced (about 1 cup)
1 jar (about 32 ounces) plain spaghetti sauce
1 can (19 ounces) chick-peas, rinsed and drained
½ cup coarsely chopped pitted ripe olives

1. Bring a large pot of water to a boil over high heat. Add rotelle and cook according to package directions, stirring frequently, until firm to the bite. Drain in a colander.

2. Meanwhile, heat oil in a Dutch oven over medium-high heat. Add carrots and cook 1 minute, stirring constantly, until coated with oil. Reduce heat to medium-low, cover and cook 4 to 5 minutes, until crisp-tender.

3. Stir spaghetti sauce, chick-peas and olives into Dutch oven. Raise heat to high and bring to a boil. Reduce heat to medium-low, cover and simmer 5 to 7 minutes, until carrots are tender.

4. Transfer rotelle to a large heated serving bowl. Pour sauce over pasta; toss to coat and serve.

Makes 4 servings, 5 cups sauce. Per serving: 820 calories, 26 grams protein, 142 grams carbohydrate, 15 grams fat, 0 milligrams cholesterol, 1,670 milligrams sodium

---

Canned Beans

☐ High-protein beans are an excellent meat substitute, especially when combined with the complex carbohydrates of pasta and protein-rich cheese. Beans are also a good source of dietary fiber.

☐ Avoid canned beans packed with sugar or dextrose; while sugar may help retain the beans' shape, it adds an undesirable sweet taste.

☐ Follow recipe instructions for draining the beans. In some recipes the liquid is used; it helps to provide moisture and thicken the sauce and may retain some of the fiber and vitamins from the beans.

Pasta and Pinto Beans Alfredo

Pasta and Pinto Beans Alfredo

Serve immediately, before the pasta absorbs the sauce (if it does, stir in a little milk). Tomato wedges drizzled with oil and vinegar are a good accompaniment.

8 ounces capellini (angel-hair pasta),
    broken in half
2 tablespoons butter or margarine
1 teaspoon minced fresh garlic
3 cups frozen carrots and peas (from a
    20-ounce bag)
1 can (about 16 ounces) pinto beans,
    drained
1 cup half-and-half
½ cup grated Parmesan cheese
½ teaspoon salt

1. Bring a large pot of water to a boil over high heat. Add capellini and cook according to package directions, stirring frequently, until firm to the bite. Drain in a colander.

2. Meanwhile, melt butter in a large skillet over medium heat. Add garlic and cook 30 seconds, stirring constantly, just until tender but not browned. Add carrots and peas and pinto beans. Raise heat to medium-high and cook 3 minutes, stirring occasionally, until carrots and peas are nearly crisp-tender.

3. Reduce heat under skillet to medium-low. Add half-and-half, Parmesan cheese and salt. Stir about 2 minutes, until hot (do not boil).

4. Transfer capellini to a large heated serving bowl. Pour sauce over pasta; toss to mix and serve immediately.

Makes 4 servings. Per serving: 540 calories, 24 grams protein, 73 grams carbohydrate, 17 grams fat, 56 milligrams cholesterol with butter, 38 milligrams cholesterol with margarine, 538 milligrams sodium

Spaghetti with Chick-pea Sauce

A dish for garlic lovers.

1 **pound thin spaghetti**
½ **cup olive oil**
4 **cloves garlic, minced**
1 **large bay leaf**
1 **can (20 ounces) chick-peas,**
    undrained
½ **teaspoon dried thyme leaves**
½ **teaspoon salt**
Pepper to taste

1. Bring a large pot of water to a boil over high heat. Add spaghetti and cook according to package directions, stirring frequently, until firm to the bite. Drain in a colander.

2. Meanwhile, heat oil in a medium-size saucepan over medium-high heat. Add garlic and bay leaf and cook, stirring constantly, until garlic is light golden brown.

3. Stir chick-peas, thyme, salt and pepper into saucepan. Bring to a boil and boil 3 minutes, until sauce is reduced and thickened slightly. If you like a thicker sauce, mash some of the chick-peas against the side of the saucepan.

4. Transfer spaghetti to a large heated serving bowl. Pour in sauce; toss to coat and serve immediately.

Makes 4 servings. Per serving: 847 calories, 22 grams protein, 118 grams carbohydrate, 30 grams fat, 0 milligrams cholesterol, 706 milligrams sodium

Cheesy Macaroni, Spinach and Beans

A welcome change from the usual.

3 **tablespoons vegetable oil**
1 **medium onion, chopped**
2 **large cloves garlic, minced**
¼ **teaspoon crushed red-pepper flakes,**
    or to taste
4 **cups water**
1 **teaspoon salt**
1 **package (7¼ ounces) macaroni-and-**
    cheese mix (reserve sauce mix)
1 **package (10 ounces) frozen chopped**
    spinach
1 **can (15½ ounces) red kidney beans,**
    drained

1. Heat oil in a large heavy skillet over medium-high heat. Add onion, garlic and crushed red pepper and cook about 3 minutes, until onion is golden.

2. Add water and salt. Cover and bring to a boil. Stir in macaroni and simmer 5 minutes, stirring a few times.

3. Stir in spinach and cook until broken up, stirring a few times. Stir in beans and reserved sauce mix until well blended. Reduce heat to medium and simmer 5 minutes, until beans and spinach are hot and macaroni is firm to the bite.

4. Transfer to a medium-size heated serving bowl or serve from skillet.

Makes 4 servings. Per serving: 366 calories, 16 grams protein, 55 grams carbohydrate, 10 grams fat, 0 milligrams cholesterol, 887 milligrams sodium

Mushrooms

🕐 **MAKE-AHEAD**
♥ **LOW-CALORIE**
✳ **MICROWAVE**

Eggplant-Mushroom Sauce

This hearty meatless sauce is lower in calories than most pasta sauces. Serve over freshly cooked pasta and pass Parmesan cheese at the table.

  1 large onion, chopped (about 1 cup)
1½ teaspoons minced fresh garlic
  2 tablespoons olive or vegetable oil
  1 can (28 ounces) tomatoes, drained;
      1 cup juice reserved and
      tomatoes broken up
  1 eggplant (about 1¼ pounds), cut in
      ¾-inch cubes (about 8 cups)
  4 ounces mushrooms, sliced (about
      2 cups)
  ¼ cup Marsala or medium-sweet
      Madeira wine or water
  1 teaspoon dried oregano leaves
  1 teaspoon dried basil leaves
  ¾ teaspoon salt
  ¼ teaspoon pepper

1. Stir onion, garlic and oil in a deep, 3-quart microwave-safe bowl or baking dish. Microwave on high 2 minutes, until onion is crisp-tender.

2. Add tomatoes, eggplant, mushrooms, Marsala, herbs and salt and pepper; toss to mix. Cover tightly with a lid or vented plastic wrap. Microwave on high 10 minutes; stir.

3. Uncover and microwave on high 12 to 15 minutes, stirring every 5 minutes, until sauce thickens and eggplant is tender. Serve immediately over freshly cooked pasta or cover and refrigerate until ready to serve. Reheat in microwave on high before serving.

Makes 6 cups sauce, four 1½-cup servings. Per serving of sauce (with Marsala): 155 calories, 5 grams protein, 20 grams carbohydrate, 8 grams fat, 0 milligrams cholesterol, 668 milligrams sodium

Pasta with Mushrooms and Nuts

The nuts add a wonderful crunch. Use freshly grated Parmesan cheese if possible.

  8 ounces rotelle (about 4 cups)
  3 tablespoons olive oil
  ½ cup chopped onion
  2 teaspoons minced fresh garlic
  4 ounces mushrooms, sliced (about
      2 cups)
  1 cup coarsely chopped pecans or
      walnuts (4 ounces)
  1 cup frozen green peas
  ½ cup small pitted ripe olives, halved
  ½ cup minced fresh parsley
  ¾ cup grated Parmesan cheese

1. Bring a large pot of water to a boil over high heat. Add rotelle and cook according to package directions, stirring frequently, until firm to the bite. Drain in a colander.

2. Meanwhile, heat oil in a large skillet over medium-high heat. Add onion and garlic and cook 3 minutes, stirring occasionally, until onion is nearly tender.

3. Stir mushrooms into skillet and cook 2 minutes. Add pecans, peas, olives and parsley and cook 3 minutes, stirring frequently, until heated through.

4. Transfer rotelle to a large heated serving bowl. Spoon sauce over pasta and sprinkle with cheese. Toss to mix and serve immediately.

Makes 4 servings. Per serving: 640 calories, 20 grams protein, 56 grams carbohydrate, 39 grams fat, 18 milligrams cholesterol, 329 milligrams sodium

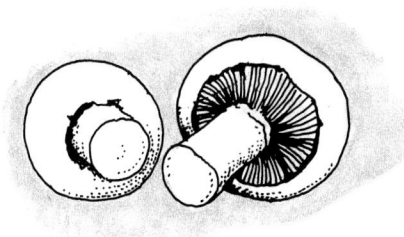

Pasta with Fresh Mushroom Sauce

The delicate flavor of this creamy sauce is the perfect complement to fettuccine. The dish is rich; serve as a first course for four or a main course for two.

- 2 tablespoons butter or margarine
- ¼ cup finely chopped shallots or green onions
- 8 ounces mushrooms, thinly sliced (about 4 cups)
- ⅓ cup Madeira wine (optional)
- 1 cup heavy cream
- 9 ounces fresh or 6 ounces dry fettuccine
- 1 tablespoon finely chopped fresh parsley
- 1 tablespoon snipped fresh chives (optional)
- ½ teaspoon salt, or to taste
- ⅛ teaspoon pepper, or to taste

1. Melt butter in a medium-size heavy saucepan over medium-high heat. Add shallots and mushrooms. Cook 4 to 5 minutes, stirring two or three times, until mushrooms release their liquid.

2. Add Madeira, if desired, and increase heat to high. Boil about 4 minutes, until 1 tablespoon liquid remains. Add cream and bring to a boil. Reduce heat to medium. Simmer 5 to 7 minutes, until sauce thickens.

3. Meanwhile, bring a large pot of water to a boil over high heat. Add fettuccine and cook according to package directions, stirring frequently, until firm to the bite. Drain in a colander and transfer to a large heated serving bowl.

4. Stir parsley, chives, if desired, salt and pepper into sauce. Pour sauce over pasta and toss to coat. Serve immediately.

Makes 2 main-dish or 4 appetizer servings. Per main-dish serving (with fresh pasta): 1,064 calories, 22 grams protein, 103 grams carbohydrate, 63 grams fat, 312 milligrams cholesterol with butter, 276 milligrams cholesterol with margarine, 738 milligrams sodium

Pasta with Fresh Mushroom Sauce

Fresh Mushrooms

☐ Fresh mushrooms add elegance to any dish, especially pasta. Purchase firm, smooth mushrooms.

☐ Store prepacked mushrooms unwashed in their original container in the refrigerator until ready to use. Once the package is opened, or if you've purchased the mushrooms loose, keep them in a paper bag to ensure freshness. Plastic bags cause mushrooms to sweat and deteriorate faster. Properly stored, mushrooms will keep fresh for several days.

☐ Mushrooms absorb water just like little sponges, so don't soak them to clean them. Either wipe them with a damp paper towel or rinse them quickly with cool water.

☐ The white button mushroom is the most commonly available, but look for exotic varieties in your market's produce aisle. Exotics can be substituted for white mushrooms to add flair to any of our recipes. Some of the types now available include:

Shiitake: A large, open-capped mushroom with a full-bodied taste. Wonderful in recipes including garlic, hot peppers or wine.

Oyster: Light beige or soft brown with a shell or trumpet shape. They are very delicate in flavor and rather fragile.

Crimini or Italian Brown: Light tan to dark brown in color, they are a cousin to the familiar white mushroom but with a richer, earthier flavor.

Pasta with Meat or Poultry

These robust classic dishes show just how delicious pasta with chicken, turkey, salami, Italian sausage, prosciutto or bacon can be.

Spaghetti with Meatballs and Vegetables

Beef

Spaghetti with Meatballs and Vegetables

Meatballs
½ cup packaged seasoned dry
    bread crumbs
¼ cup water
12 ounces lean ground beef
1 large egg
1 tablespoon olive or vegetable oil

Sauce and Spaghetti
1 cup frozen or fresh chopped onion
8 ounces zucchini, halved lengthwise
    and cut crosswise in ½-inch pieces
    (about 1 cup)
1 medium-size bell pepper (yellow,
    red or green), cut in ½-inch pieces,
    or 1 cup frozen chopped green
    bell pepper
1 box (10 ounces) frozen
    broccoli florets
1 box (10 ounces) frozen
    cauliflower florets
1 jar (about 32 ounces) plain
    spaghetti sauce
1 cup cherry tomatoes (6 ounces),
    halved
1 pound spaghetti

1. To make meatballs, stir bread crumbs and water in a medium-size bowl. Let stand 3 minutes to soften.

2. Add ground beef and egg and mix until well blended. Form level tablespoonfuls into 1-inch balls (you will have about 24 meatballs).

3. Heat oil in a large Dutch oven over medium-high heat. Add meatballs in a single layer. Cook 8 to 10 minutes, shaking or stirring three or four times, until meatballs are browned and barely pink in centers. Remove to a plate with a slotted spoon.

4. To make sauce, stir onion, zucchini and bell pepper into Dutch oven. Cook 3 to 5 minutes, until vegetables are crisp-tender. Add broccoli and cauliflower and cook about 5 minutes, stirring often, until florets are separated.

5. Gently stir in spaghetti sauce, meatballs and cherry tomatoes and bring to a boil. Reduce heat to medium-low, cover and simmer 8 to 10 minutes, stirring twice, until meatballs are firm and vegetables are tender.

6. Meanwhile, bring a large pot of water to a boil over high heat. Add spaghetti and cook according to package directions, stirring frequently, until firm to the bite. Drain in a colander.

7. Transfer spaghetti to a large heated serving platter. Spoon meatballs and sauce over pasta. Serve immediately.

Makes 4 servings, 8 cups meatballs and sauce. Per serving (with 6 meatballs): 1,017 calories, 44 grams protein, 140 grams carbohydrate, 31 grams fat, 122 milligrams cholesterol, 1,728 milligrams sodium

Shells with Beef, Carrots and Red Wine

A hearty dish, just the thing on a chilly day. Serve with a salad of sliced cucumbers and red onion, ripe olives and Italian dressing. Fresh apples make a perfect dessert.

1 pound medium-size pasta shells
1 tablespoon olive or vegetable oil
2 medium-size carrots, scrubbed and
    diced (about 1 cup)
1 medium-size stalk celery, thinly
    sliced (about ½ cup)
½ cup frozen or fresh chopped onion
12 ounces lean ground beef
⅓ cup dry red wine or water
1 jar (about 32 ounces) plain
    spaghetti sauce

1. Bring a large pot of water to a boil over high heat. Add pasta shells and cook according to package directions, stirring frequently, until firm to the bite. Drain in a colander.

2. Meanwhile, heat oil in a Dutch oven over medium-high heat. Add carrots, celery and onion and cook 5 to 6 minutes, stirring frequently, until vegetables are crisp-tender.

3. Crumble beef over vegetables and cook 3 minutes, stirring constantly, until beef is no longer pink. Add wine and boil 1 minute.

4. Stir spaghetti sauce into Dutch oven and bring to a boil. Reduce heat to medium-low. Cover and simmer 4 to 5 minutes, stirring once, until vegetables are tender.

5. Transfer pasta shells to a large heated serving bowl. Pour sauce over pasta; toss to coat and serve.

Makes 4 servings, 5½ cups sauce. Per serving (with wine): 915 calories, 36 grams protein, 124 grams carbohydrate, 28 grams fat, 58 milligrams cholesterol, 1,636 milligrams sodium

Pasta Shells with Bolognese Sauce

Pasta Shells with Bolognese Sauce

Serve with plenty of Italian bread and a salad of roasted red peppers (from a jar) and mozzarella cheese dressed with oil and vinegar.

12 ounces small pasta shells (about 4 cups)
2 tablespoons olive or vegetable oil
1 cup frozen or fresh chopped onion
2 teaspoons minced fresh garlic
1 pound lean ground beef
1 can (29 ounces) tomato purée (salt-free)
1 tablespoon dried basil leaves
1½ teaspoons dried oregano leaves
1 teaspoon salt
¼ teaspoon pepper
Chopped fresh parsley (optional)
Coarsely shredded Parmesan cheese (optional)

1. Bring a large pot of water to a boil over high heat. Add pasta shells and cook according to package directions, stirring frequently, until firm to the bite. Drain in a colander

2. Meanwhile, heat oil in a large saucepan over high heat. Add onion and garlic and cook 3 minutes, stirring occasionally, until onion is nearly tender. Crumble beef into saucepan and cook about 3 minutes, stirring frequently, until no longer pink.

3. Stir tomato purée, herbs, salt and pepper into saucepan. Bring to a boil. Reduce heat to low and simmer 8 minutes, until flavors have blended.

4. Spoon pasta into bowls and top with sauce. Sprinkle with parsley and Parmesan, if desired, and serve.

Makes 4 servings. Per serving: 703 calories, 35 grams protein, 86 grams carbohydrate, 25 grams fat, 77 milligrams cholesterol, 648 milligrams sodium

Ragu Sauce

Ragu is a thick sauce with little bits of meat in it; in this recipe we used ground beef. It is good with spaghetti, ziti or shells or in a baked lasagne. This sauce makes enough for four to six servings and can be frozen.

- 3 tablespoons olive oil
- 3 tablespoons butter or margarine
- ½ cup chopped onion
- 1 clove garlic, crushed
- 1 pound lean ground beef
- ½ cup dry red wine
- 1 cup canned tomato purée, preferably made with plum tomatoes
- 1 cup chicken broth
- ½ teaspoon salt
- ¼ teaspoon ground nutmeg
- Pepper to taste

1. Heat oil and butter in a Dutch oven over medium-high heat. Add onion and garlic and cook, stirring occasionally, until onion is tender. Stir in meat and cook, stirring occasionally, until no longer pink.

2. Stir in wine; increase heat slightly and cook, stirring occasionally, until half the wine has evaporated.

3. Stir in purée, broth, salt, nutmeg and pepper. Bring to a boil. Reduce heat to low. Cover and simmer 1 hour, stirring occasionally.

4. Uncover and simmer until sauce is desired thickness. Serve immediately over freshly cooked pasta, or cool and refrigerate or freeze. Skim off fat and reheat when ready to use.

Makes about 3 cups. Per ½ cup: 308 calories, 15 grams protein, 8 grams carbohydrate, 24 grams fat, 71 milligrams cholesterol with butter, 53 milligrams cholesterol with margarine, 675 milligrams sodium

One-Arm Pasta Sauce

This sauce is a mainstay in the busy household of Debbi Fields (of Mrs. Fields's Cookies fame). Serve hot over freshly cooked spaghetti, bow ties or twists, sprinkled with freshly grated Parmesan cheese. Leftover sauce can be refrigerated up to a week; freeze for longer storage.

- 2 pounds lean ground beef
- 2 medium-size onions, chopped
- 2 teaspoons minced fresh garlic
- 1 can (28 ounces) tomatoes
- 2 cans (8 ounces each) tomato sauce
- 1 cup dry red wine
- 10 to 12 ounces mushrooms, sliced
- 1 teaspoon salt, or to taste
- 1 teaspoon anise seed, or to taste
- 1 teaspoon dried basil leaves
- 1 teaspoon dried oregano leaves
- ½ teaspoon pepper
- 2 bay leaves

1. Place meat in a large Dutch oven and pile onions and garlic on top. Cook over medium heat, breaking up meat with a wooden spoon, until no longer pink. Stir well and cook until meat and onions are lightly browned. Remove excess fat with a bulb-baster or a spoon.

2. Add remaining ingredients to Dutch oven; stir well. Cover and bring to a boil. Reduce heat to low and simmer 30 to 40 minutes, stirring occasionally. If sauce is too thin, uncover and simmer briskly just until thickened. If it's too thick, stir in water or additional wine. Discard bay leaves.

Makes about 8 cups. Per ½ cup: 149 calories, 12 grams protein, 7 grams carbohydrate, 8 grams fat, 38 milligrams cholesterol, 419 milligrams sodium

Sugo Di Spuntature

Served over rigatoni, this delicious sauce is made with ribs and Italian sausage (*spuntature* means bits and pieces of meat). Pass grated Parmesan cheese at the table. Sauce can be made up to four days ahead and kept refrigerated. Reheat before serving.

2½ pounds beef short ribs or country-
    style pork ribs or pork spareribs
1 tablespoon dried basil leaves
1 tablespoon dried oregano leaves
1½ teaspoons pepper
1 teaspoon salt
2 tablespoons olive oil
1½ pounds beef chuck for stew, cut in
    ¾-inch pieces
1 pound sweet or hot Italian sausage,
    cut in 2-inch lengths
1½ cups finely chopped onions
1 tablespoon minced fresh garlic
Three 1½-inch-long bay leaves
¼ teaspoon crushed red-pepper flakes
1 cup dry red wine (optional)
1 can (35 ounces) Italian plum
    tomatoes, puréed in blender or
    food processor, or 2 cans (16
    ounces each) tomato sauce
1½ pounds rigatoni

1. Heat oven to 350°F.

2. Put ribs in a 13x9-inch baking dish. Sprinkle with basil, oregano, ½ teaspoon of the pepper and the salt. Bake 1 hour, until ribs are well browned and meat is almost tender.

3. While ribs bake, heat oil in a Dutch oven or a large heavy pot over medium-high heat. Stir in beef, sausage, onions, garlic, bay leaves, remaining 1 teaspoon pepper and the crushed red pepper. Cook until meat is brown, stirring often.

4. Add wine to Dutch oven, if desired, and boil about 1 minute, stirring to scrape up the browned bits from the bottom. Stir in tomatoes and bring to a boil. Add ribs; return to a boil and reduce heat to low. (Sauce will be very thin at this point.)

5. Simmer 1½ to 2 hours, until sauce is thick and meat is tender. Remove from heat. Remove bay leaves. Skim off fat.

6. Bring a large pot of water to a boil over high heat. Add rigatoni and cook according to package directions, stirring frequently, until firm to the bite. Drain in a colander.

7. Spoon rigatoni onto plates. Spoon sauce over pasta, placing a rib and some beef and sausage on each plate. Serve immediately.

Makes 6 generous servings. Per serving: 1,176 calories, 62 grams protein, 98 grams carbohydrate, 58 grams fat, 174 milligrams cholesterol, 1,254 milligrams sodium

Ground-Beef Stroganoff

On the side: mixed greens tossed with a simple oil-vinegar dressing.

1 tablespoon vegetable oil
8 ounces lean ground beef
2¼ cups water
1 cup milk
½ cup frozen or fresh chopped green
    bell pepper
1 envelope (from 2.5-ounce box)
    onion-soup mix
¼ teaspoon salt
Pepper to taste
6 ounces capellini (angel-hair pasta),
    broken in thirds
2 cups mixed frozen green peas and
    sliced carrots

1. Heat oil in a large skillet (preferably nonstick) over high heat. Add beef and cook 3 minutes, stirring to break up pieces, until meat is no longer pink.

2. Add 2 cups of the water, the milk, bell pepper, soup mix, salt and pepper. Stir to mix well. Scatter pasta over top. Cover and bring to a boil. Boil 2 minutes, stirring three times with a fork to separate strands of pasta.

3. Stir in peas and carrots. Cover and reduce heat to low. Simmer 4 minutes, until vegetables and pasta are tender. Stir in remaining ¼ cup water and remove from heat. Serve immediately.

Makes 4 servings. Per serving: 357 calories, 13 grams protein, 51 grams carbohydrate, 7 grams fat, 25 milligrams cholesterol, 978 milligrams sodium

Chicken

⏱ **MAKE-AHEAD**
★ **SPECIAL—AND WORTH IT**

Grilled Chicken with Fettuccine in Mushroom and Pepper Sauce

For a very special meal, make this with fresh exotic mushrooms, but white mushrooms are delicious, too. Make sure the bell peppers are firm and thick-walled. You can prepare most of this dish ahead, making it a good choice for entertaining.

½ cup olive oil
½ cup minced fresh basil leaves
3 tablespoons lemon juice
½ to 1 teaspoon crushed red-pepper
    flakes
2 teaspoons minced fresh garlic
1½ pounds boned chicken-breast
    halves
1 *each* medium-size red and yellow
    bell pepper
3 tablespoons unsalted butter or
    margarine
½ cup dry white wine
½ cup chicken broth
2 cups heavy cream
4 ounces medium-size mushrooms,
    quartered (about 1 cup)
½ teaspoon salt
12 ounces fettuccine
½ cup freshly grated Parmesan cheese

1. Mix oil, ¼ cup of the basil, the lemon juice, crushed red pepper and garlic in a shallow dish. Add chicken and turn to coat. Cover and marinate in refrigerator at least 3 hours or overnight.

2. To make sauce: Peel sides of bell peppers with a vegetable peeler. Reserve skins and cut peppers in very thin strips.

3. Melt 1½ tablespoons of the butter in a small saucepan over low heat. Add bell-pepper peels and cook 2 minutes, until tender. Stir in wine and chicken broth. Increase heat to high and boil about 5 minutes, until only about 1 tablespoon liquid is left.

4. Add cream and cook 4 minutes, stirring constantly, until mixture is reduced by half and thick enough to coat the back of a metal spoon. Remove from heat.

5. Melt remaining 1½ tablespoons butter in a large skillet over medium-high heat. Add mushrooms and cook about 2 minutes, until browned.

6. Pour cream sauce through a strainer into skillet. Remove from heat. Stir in salt, then pepper strips. Cover and keep warm. (Can be refrigerated at this point. Warm mixture over low heat when ready to use.)

7. To cook chicken: Turn on broiler. Drain chicken; discard marinade. Arrange chicken on broiler-pan rack. Broil 4 inches from heat source 5 minutes per side, just until no longer pink in the center and juices run clear when chicken is pierced.

8. Meanwhile, bring a large pot of water to a boil over high heat. Add fettuccine and cook according to package directions, stirring frequently, until firm to the bite. Drain in a colander and transfer to a large heated serving bowl.

9. Discard chicken skin and cut meat in chunks. Add to hot pasta in bowl.

10. Stir cheese and remaining ¼ cup basil into warm sauce. Pour over chicken and pasta. Toss to mix and serve immediately.

Makes 4 servings. Per serving: 870 calories, 59 grams protein, 42 grams carbohydrate, 25 grams fat, 303 milligrams cholesterol with butter, 276 milligrams cholesterol with margarine, 576 milligrams sodium

Grilled Chicken with Fettuccine in Mushroom and Pepper Sauce

Bok Choy with Linguine and Sesame Sauce

Bok Choy with Linguine and Sesame Sauce

Oriental sesame oil is dark brown because the sesame seed is toasted. Store it in the refrigerator for freshness. It is found in the Oriental-food section of supermarkets and in specialty stores.

6 ounces boned and skinned chicken-breast halves, cut in narrow strips
3 tablespoons dry sherry
½ teaspoon minced fresh garlic
⅛ teaspoon pepper
8 ounces linguine
3 tablespoons soy sauce
1 tablespoon Oriental sesame oil (optional)
½ teaspoon granulated sugar
5 tablespoons vegetable oil
½ cup chopped green onions
1¼ pounds bok choy, shredded (about 4 packed cups)
1 tablespoon toasted sesame seed (see Note)

1. Put chicken, 1 tablespoon of the sherry, the garlic and pepper in a small bowl. Mix well; cover and marinate 15 minutes, stirring once or twice.

2. Bring a large pot of water to a boil over high heat. Add linguine and cook according to package directions, stirring frequently, until firm to the bite. Drain in a colander.

3. Meanwhile, mix remaining 2 tablespoons sherry, the soy sauce, sesame oil, if desired, and sugar in a small bowl. Set aside.

4. Heat 2 tablespoons of the vegetable oil in a wok or a large skillet over medium-high heat. Add chicken and ¼ cup of the green onions. Cook 1 to 2 minutes, stirring constantly, just until chicken turns white. Remove to a small bowl.

5. Add remaining 3 tablespoons vegetable oil and the bok choy to skillet. Stir-fry 2 minutes, stirring constantly. Add linguine and cook 1 minute longer, stirring constantly. Add soy-sauce mixture, chicken mixture and remaining ¼ cup green onions to wok. Toss well to coat and cook until heated through. Sprinkle with sesame seed, transfer to a heated platter or large serving bowl and serve immediately.

Makes 4 servings. Per serving (without sesame oil): 529 calories, 33 grams protein, 50 grams carbohydrate, 22 grams fat, 56 milligrams cholesterol, 1,070 milligrams sodium

Note: To toast sesame seed, shake in a skillet over medium-high heat until seeds are browned and start to pop. Transfer to a plate or bowl immediately; otherwise seeds will continue to cook in the hot skillet.

Chicken-Liver Lo Mein Dinner

Halved broccoli florets or sliced stems, or shredded cabbage and sliced carrots and celery can be substituted for the green beans. Strips of chicken or pork can be used instead of livers.

    8 ounces thin spaghetti such as
          vermicelli
   12 ounces chicken livers (halve large
          ones), trimmed and patted dry
Pepper to taste
    4 tablespoons vegetable oil
    1 large clove garlic, halved
    8 ounces small green beans, trimmed
          and broken in halves (about
          1½ cups)
    4 ounces mushrooms, sliced
          (about 2 cups)
   ¾ cup chicken broth
   ¼ cup soy sauce
   ½ cup sliced green onions

1. Bring a large pot of water to a boil over high heat. Add spaghetti and cook according to package directions, stirring frequently, until firm to the bite. Drain in a colander.

2. Season livers with pepper.

3. Heat 2 tablespoons of the oil in a very large skillet or wok over medium-high heat. Add garlic and cook until lightly browned; remove and discard. Add livers and cook 4 minutes, stirring frequently, until browned. Remove livers to a plate with a slotted spoon.

4. Heat remaining 2 tablespoons oil in skillet. Add beans and mushrooms and cook 3 to 4 minutes, stirring constantly, until beans are crisp-tender.

5. Stir in chicken broth, soy sauce, green onions and livers. Cover and cook 2 minutes. Add spaghetti and toss gently to mix. Cook 1 minute, just until hot. Serve immediately.

Makes 4 servings. Per serving: 427 calories, 32 grams protein, 33 grams carbohydrate, 19 grams fat, 704 milligrams cholesterol, 1,530 milligrams sodium

Pasta with Chicken Livers Marinara

Liver is an excellent source of iron.

    8 ounces thin linguine
    3 tablespoons olive oil
    1 pound chicken livers (halve large
          ones), trimmed
   ½ teaspoon minced fresh garlic
    1 can (28 ounces) tomatoes, drained
          and tomatoes cut up
    2 cups frozen green peas
  1½ teaspoons dried basil leaves
   ¼ teaspoon pepper

1. Bring a large pot of water to a boil over high heat. Add linguine and cook according to package directions, stirring frequently, until firm to the bite. Drain in a colander and toss with 1 tablespoon of the oil to prevent sticking.

2. Meanwhile, heat remaining 2 tablespoons oil in a large skillet over medium-high heat. Add livers and garlic and cook 2 to 3 minutes, stirring frequently, until livers are browned outside but still very pink inside.

3. Stir in tomatoes, peas, basil and pepper. Bring to a simmer and reduce heat to medium-low. Cook 4 to 5 minutes, until flavors have blended and livers are slightly pink inside.

4. Transfer pasta to a large heated serving bowl. Spoon sauce over pasta and serve immediately.

Makes 4 servings. Per serving: 580 calories, 43 grams protein, 64 grams carbohydrate, 16 grams fat, 846 milligrams cholesterol, 422 milligrams sodium

Pasta with Chicken Livers Marinara

Turkey

Turkey Lo Mein

A fine way to use leftover turkey, but you could use chicken or pork instead.

     8 ounces thin spaghetti
    ½ cup chicken broth
     2 tablespoons soy sauce
  1½ tablespoons cornstarch
     1 teaspoon minced fresh garlic
    10 ounces cooked turkey, cut in thin
         strips (about 2 cups)
     2 tablespoons vegetable oil
     1 medium-size red or green bell
         pepper, coarsely chopped
         (about ¾ cup)
     4 medium-size green onions, thinly
         sliced (about ½ cup)
     1 box (8 ounces) frozen
         sugar-snap peas

1. Bring a large pot of water to a boil over high heat. Add spaghetti and cook according to package directions, stirring frequently, until firm to the bite. Drain in a colander.

2. Mix chicken broth, soy sauce, cornstarch and garlic in a medium-size bowl. Add turkey and toss to coat.

3. Heat oil in a Dutch oven over medium-high heat. Add bell pepper, green onions and sugar-snap peas. Stir-fry 4 to 5 minutes, until vegetables are crisp-tender.

4. Toss turkey again. Add to vegetables and bring to a boil; boil 1 minute. Stir in cooked spaghetti and toss gently to mix and coat. Cook 1 to 2 minutes to heat spaghetti, if needed.

5. Transfer to a large heated serving bowl and serve immediately.

Makes 4 servings. Per serving: 464 calories, 32 grams protein, 55 grams carbohydrate, 12 grams fat, 64 milligrams cholesterol, 853 milligrams sodium

Fettuccine with Turkey-Mushroom Sauce

For this savory sauce, use leftover cooked poultry or buy it already cooked at the deli counter.

     1 pound fettuccine, plain or spinach
     1 tablespoon olive or vegetable oil
     6 ounces mushrooms, cut in ¼-inch
         slices (about 3 cups)
     1 cup chopped celery
     1 cup frozen or fresh chopped green
         bell pepper
     1 jar (about 32 ounces) plain
         spaghetti sauce
    10 ounces cooked turkey or
         chicken, torn in small shreds
         (about 2 cups)

1. Bring a large pot of water to a boil over high heat. Add fettuccine and cook according to package directions, stirring frequently, until firm to the bite. Drain in a colander.

2. Meanwhile, heat oil in a Dutch oven over medium-high heat. Add mushrooms, celery and bell pepper and cook 3 to 5 minutes, stirring frequently, until vegetables are nearly tender.

3. Stir in spaghetti sauce and turkey and bring to a boil. Reduce heat to medium-low. Cover and simmer 6 to 8 minutes, stirring twice, until vegetables are tender.

4. Transfer fettuccine to a large heated serving bowl. Pour sauce over pasta; toss to coat and serve.

Makes 4 servings, 5½ cups sauce. Per serving: 800 calories, 43 grams protein, 120 grams carbohydrate, 14 grams fat, 63 milligrams cholesterol, 1,681 milligrams sodium

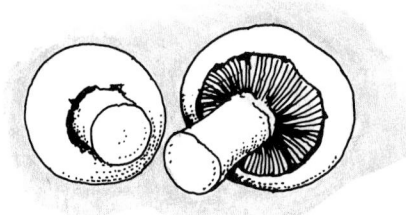

Spaghetti with Ground Turkey and Tomato Sauce

Using ground turkey instead of sausage meat reduces calories and fat. Make this sauce ahead of time, if you wish, and refrigerate or freeze until ready to use. Reheat to serve.

8 ounces ground turkey
1 teaspoon vegetable oil
½ cup chopped onion
1 teaspoon minced fresh garlic
1 can (28 ounces) tomatoes
1 can (6 ounces) tomato paste
1 cup water
1 bay leaf
1 teaspoon chopped fresh parsley
½ teaspoon dried basil leaves
½ teaspoon dried oregano leaves
½ teaspoon salt
¼ teaspoon granulated sugar
Pepper to taste
8 ounces spaghetti

1. Crumble turkey into a large nonstick saucepan or Dutch oven over medium-high heat. Cook turkey, stirring occasionally, until no longer pink. Drain meat on a paper towel.

2. Add oil, onion and garlic to saucepan and cook 3 minutes, stirring frequently, until onion is nearly tender.

3. Return turkey to saucepan. Add tomatoes, tomato paste, water, bay leaf, parsley, basil, oregano, salt and sugar. Break up tomatoes with the back of a wooden spoon. Raise heat to high and bring to a boil. Reduce heat to low. Partially cover and simmer 1½ to 2 hours, until sauce has thickened to desired consistency. Remove from heat; discard bay leaf. Season with pepper.

4. Bring a large pot of water to a boil over high heat. Add spaghetti and cook according to package directions, stirring frequently, until firm to the bite. Drain in a colander and transfer to a medium-size heated serving bowl. Spoon sauce over spaghetti and serve.

Makes 4 servings. Per serving: 388 calories, 25 grams protein, 62 grams carbohydrate, 4 grams fat, 35 milligrams cholesterol, 578 milligrams sodium

Fettuccine with Creamy Smoked-Turkey Sauce

A simple but elegant sauce coats ribbons of fettuccine. This makes a wonderful appetizer for four or a main dish for two.

9 ounces fresh or 6 ounces dry
    fettuccine
2 tablespoons finely chopped shallots
    or green onion
¼ cup dry white wine or dry vermouth
    or water
½ teaspoon balsamic or red-wine
    vinegar
1 cup heavy cream
3 ounces smoked turkey breast, cut in
    thin strips (about ¾ cup)
⅓ cup grated Parmesan cheese
Salt to taste
2 tablespoons finely chopped
    fresh parsley
Pepper to taste

1. Bring a large pot of water to a boil over high heat. Add fettuccine and cook according to package directions, stirring frequently, until firm to the bite. Drain in a colander.

2. Meanwhile, put shallots, wine and vinegar in a medium-size saucepan and bring to a boil over high heat. Boil 3 to 4 minutes, until 1 tablespoon liquid is left. Add cream; reduce heat to medium and bring to a boil. Boil 5 minutes or until thickened and reduced to about ⅔ cup.

3. Add turkey to saucepan and reduce heat to low. Simmer 1 minute. Stir in cheese until smooth. Remove from heat; taste and, if necessary, season with salt.

4. Transfer fettuccine to a heated serving bowl. Pour sauce over pasta and toss to mix. Sprinkle with parsley and season to taste with pepper. Serve immediately.

Makes 2 main-dish or 4 appetizer servings. Per main-dish serving (with fresh pasta): 1,002 calories, 28 grams protein, 97 grams carbohydrate, 56 grams fat, 296 milligrams cholesterol, 320 milligrams sodium

Ham

Rotelle with Creamy Ham and Cheese Sauce

Cooking pasta this way seems to defy the rules, but it works beautifully.

> 3 cups milk
> 1 can (11 ounces) condensed Cheddar cheese soup, undiluted
> 1 tablespoon prepared mustard
> Dash ground red pepper
> 2 cups rotelle or other large spiral pasta
> 3 cups small broccoli florets (from a 1¼-pound bunch; save stems for another use)
> 12 ounces fully cooked ham, cut in strips

1. Mix milk, soup, mustard and ground red pepper in a large deep skillet until blended and smooth. Bring to a boil over medium heat. Stir in rotelle and cook 15 minutes, stirring occasionally, until almost tender.

2. Add broccoli to skillet. Cover and simmer 10 minutes, until broccoli and pasta are tender.

3. Stir in ham and simmer just until hot. Transfer to a heated serving bowl and serve immediately.

Makes 4 servings. Per serving: 590 calories, 34 grams protein, 51 grams carbohydrate, 28 grams fat, 111 milligrams cholesterol, 1,795 milligrams sodium

Ham, Pasta and Broccoli with Peanut Sauce

A variation of the favorite Chinese sesame noodles. Round out this meal with a cucumber-and-carrot salad.

> 12 ounces vermicelli
> 8 ounces fully cooked ham, cut in thin strips (about 1½ cups)
> 1 bag (16 ounces) frozen cut broccoli
> ½ cup peanut butter, chunky or smooth
> ¼ cup cider vinegar
> ¼ cup water
> 2 tablespoons soy sauce
> 2 teaspoons dry mustard
> 1 teaspoon minced fresh garlic
> ½ teaspoon crushed red-pepper flakes
> For garnish: sliced green onions and chopped peanuts

1. Bring a large pot of water to a boil over high heat. Add vermicelli and cook according to package directions, stirring frequently, until firm to the bite. Drain in a colander.

2. Meanwhile, put ham and broccoli in a medium-size saucepan. Cover and cook over medium heat 7 to 10 minutes, stirring occasionally (no need to add liquid; enough is released by the ham and broccoli), until broccoli is heated through.

3. While pasta and broccoli cook, blend together peanut butter, vinegar, water, soy sauce, mustard, garlic and crushed red pepper in a small bowl.

4. Transfer pasta to a large heated serving bowl. Add ham and broccoli and the peanut-butter sauce and toss to coat. Sprinkle with green onions and peanuts and serve.

Makes 4 servings. Per serving (without garnish): 676 calories, 33 grams protein, 78 grams carbohydrate, 27 grams fat, 50 milligrams cholesterol, 1,570 milligrams sodium

Ham, Pasta and Broccoli with Peanut Sauce

Rotelle with Creamy Ham and Cheese Sauce

Pasta with Ham, Broccoli and Hot-Pepper Sauce

Pasta Twists with Creamy Broccoli Sauce

Ground nutmeg gives this sauce a special flavor. Use preground nutmeg, or grate a whole nutmeg for an extra burst of flavor.

    3 tablespoons olive or vegetable oil
    ½ cup frozen or fresh chopped onion
    2 teaspoons minced fresh garlic
    1 bag (20 ounces) frozen cut broccoli
    1 cup chicken broth
    8 ounces pasta twists
    1 cup milk
    8 ounces fully cooked ham, diced
    ⅛ teaspoon ground nutmeg
    ⅛ teaspoon pepper

1. Heat oil in a large saucepan over medium heat. Add onion and garlic and cook until onion is tender. Stir in broccoli and chicken broth and bring to a boil. Reduce heat to low. Cover and simmer about 18 minutes, until broccoli is very tender.

2. Meanwhile, bring a large pot of water to a boil over high heat. Add pasta twists and cook according to package directions, stirring frequently, until firm to the bite. Drain in a colander, reserving ⅓ cup of the cooking water.

3. Mash broccoli against the side of saucepan into a chunky purée. Stir in milk, ham, nutmeg and pepper. Increase heat to medium and cook 3 minutes longer, until sauce is thick and creamy. Stir in reserved pasta cooking water.

4. Transfer pasta to a large heated serving bowl. Pour sauce over pasta. Toss to coat and serve.

Makes 4 servings. Per serving: 528 calories, 25 grams protein, 55 grams carbohydrate, 23 grams fat, 61 milligrams cholesterol, 913 milligrams sodium

Pasta with Ham, Broccoli and Hot-Pepper Sauce

Prepare this super quick recipe from items in your freezer and pantry. For dessert: sliced ripe pears topped with grated semisweet chocolate.

    1 pound spaghetti
    1 tablespoon olive or vegetable oil
    1 box (10 ounces) frozen
       broccoli florets
    1 cup frozen or fresh chopped onion
    1 jar (about 32 ounces) plain
       spaghetti sauce
    8 ounces fully cooked ham, cut in ½-
       inch pieces (about 1½ cups)
    ½ teaspoon crushed red-pepper flakes,
       or to taste

1. Bring a large pot of water to a boil over high heat. Add spaghetti and cook according to package directions, stirring frequently, until firm to the bite. Drain in a colander.

2. Meanwhile, heat oil in a Dutch oven over medium-high heat. Add broccoli and onion and cook 4 to 6 minutes, stirring frequently to separate florets, until broccoli is crisp-tender.

3. Stir in spaghetti sauce, ham and crushed red pepper and bring to a boil. Reduce heat to medium-low. Cover and simmer 5 to 7 minutes, stirring twice, until broccoli is tender and ham is hot.

4. Transfer spaghetti to a large heated serving bowl or platter. Pour sauce over spaghetti; toss to coat and serve.

Makes 4 servings, 6 cups sauce. Per serving: 789 calories, 33 grams protein, 123 grams carbohydrate, 17 grams fat, 50 milligrams cholesterol, 1,741 milligrams sodium

---

Ham

☐ Ham, the cured hind leg of pork, is an excellent source of high-quality protein, thiamine and iron.

☐ The fully cooked ham used in these recipes can be taken right from the package or bought at the deli counter. It needs no special preparation before adding to the sauce or skillet.

☐ Ham is available in a wide range of saltiness, from a low-salt variety to Smithfield ham, which is intensely salty.

Artichokes and Ham Alfredo

Sliced tomatoes on lettuce or a tossed green salad and fresh fruit for dessert complete the meal. You can omit the egg yolk if you like; the sauce won't be as creamy and thick, but it will be just as delicious and lower in cholesterol and fat.

12 ounces fettuccine or linguine
¼ cup butter or margarine
½ teaspoon minced fresh garlic
1 can (14 ounces) water-packed artichoke hearts, drained and quartered
8 ounces fully cooked ham, cut in ¼-inch-thick strips (about 2 cups)
¾ cup half-and-half
Yolk from 1 large egg
½ cup grated Parmesan cheese

1. Bring a large pot of water to a boil over high heat. Add fettuccine and cook according to package directions, stirring frequently, until firm to the bite. Drain in a colander.

2. Meanwhile, melt butter in a medium-size saucepan over medium-low heat. Stir in garlic, then artichokes and ham, stirring to coat with butter. Reduce heat to low, cover and cook 5 minutes, until artichokes and ham are hot.

3. Beat half-and-half and egg yolk in a small bowl with a fork until well blended.

4. Transfer fettuccine to a large heated serving bowl. Pour egg mixture over fettuccine. Sprinkle with Parmesan and toss to coat. Add artichokes and ham and toss again. Serve immediately.

Makes 4 servings. Per serving: 373 calories, 19 grams protein, 6 grams carbohydrate, 31 grams fat, 180 milligrams cholesterol with butter, 149 milligrams cholesterol with margarine, 1,113 milligrams sodium

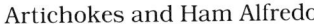
Artichokes and Ham Alfredo

Fettuccine with Ham and Artichoke Hearts

Fettuccine with Ham and Artichoke Hearts

You can use dry fettuccine instead of fresh. It takes longer to cook—about 12 minutes—so don't add the milk mixture to the sauce until the fettuccine is almost done.

- 1 **package (9 ounces) fresh fettuccine**
- 1 **tablespoon olive oil**
- 6 **ounces (half a 12-ounce package) fully cooked breakfast-ham slices, stacked, cut in quarters, then in eighths**
- 1 **package (9 ounces) frozen artichoke-heart halves and quarters, thawed**
- 8 **cherry tomatoes, halved**
- ¼ **cup sliced green onions**
- ⅓ **cup sliced ripe olives**
- ¾ **cup milk**
- ½ **cup mayonnaise**
- ½ **cup grated Parmesan cheese**

1. Bring a large pot of water to a boil over high heat. Add fettuccine and cook according to package directions, stirring frequently, until firm to the bite. Drain in a colander.

2. Meanwhile, heat oil in a large skillet over medium-high heat. Add ham and cook 5 minutes, stirring occasionally, until lightly browned.

3. Stir artichokes, cherry tomatoes, green onions and olives into skillet. Reduce heat to medium.

4. Mix milk, mayonnaise and Parmesan in a 2-cup measure until blended. Stir ham and vegetables in skillet while slowly adding mayonnaise mixture. Stir until sauce is thickened and hot. Remove from heat.

5. Transfer fettuccine to a heated serving platter. Spoon sauce over pasta and serve immediately.

Makes 4 servings. Per serving: 593 calories, 26 grams protein, 46 grams carbohydrate, 36 grams fat, 164 milligrams cholesterol, 1,040 milligrams sodium

Spaghetti Carbonara

To avoid winding up with scrambled eggs, add the egg mixture very slowly to the hot noodles, tossing them rapidly all the while. Traditional carbonara is made with bacon, but Smithfield ham tastes better and never gets flabby.

4 large eggs
2 tablespoons heavy cream
Salt and pepper to taste (depending on saltiness of meat)
8 ounces baked Smithfield ham, cut in slivers (see Note)
1 pound spaghetti
1 cup grated Parmesan cheese

1. Beat eggs with the cream, salt and pepper in a medium-size bowl. Stir in ham.

2. Bring a large pot of water to a boil over high heat. Add spaghetti and cook according to package directions, stirring frequently, until firm to the bite. Drain in a colander and immediately return to cooking pot over turned-off burner.

3. Give egg mixture another stir; then begin to pour it gently and slowly into the spaghetti, tossing all the while so that the eggs don't scramble. Add cheeses and continue tossing spaghetti until cheeses have melted.

4. Transfer to a large heated serving platter. Serve immediately with more grated cheese, if desired.

Makes 4 servings. Per serving (without additional cheese): 746 calories, 45 grams protein, 86 grams carbohydrate, 23 grams fat, 255 milligrams cholesterol, 1,485 milligrams sodium

Note: If desired, substitute ½ pound prosciutto ham, cut in slivers, or ½ pound cooked crumbled pork-sausage meat for the baked Smithfield ham.

Spaghetti with Ham and Cheddar

1 pound spaghetti
2 tablespoons butter or margarine
8 ounces fully cooked ham, cut in thin strips
1 small onion, chopped
1 can (10¾ ounces) condensed cream-of-chicken soup, undiluted
⅔ cup milk
2 tablespoons chopped fresh parsley
½ cup shredded Cheddar cheese (2 ounces)

1. Bring a large pot of water to a boil over high heat. Add spaghetti and cook according to package directions, stirring frequently, until firm to the bite. Drain in a colander.

2. Meanwhile, melt butter in a large skillet over medium-high heat. Add ham and onion and cook about 5 minutes, stirring occasionally, until ham is lightly browned.

3. Stir soup, milk and parsley into skillet; reduce heat to medium and simmer 5 minutes.

4. Transfer spaghetti to a large heated serving bowl. Pour sauce over pasta. Sprinkle with Cheddar and toss well. Serve immediately.

Makes 4 servings. Per serving: 730 calories, 35 grams protein, 94 grams carbohydrate, 23 grams fat, 76 milligrams cholesterol with butter, 61 milligrams cholesterol with margarine, 1,625 milligrams sodium

Prosciutto and Bacon

Quadrettini

Quadrettini means "little squares." Children or a guest can break or cut the fettuccine while you prepare the sauce. This dish—to be eaten with a spoon—serves two as a main course but is easily doubled for four. It is also excellent as a first course; follow with roast chicken and a green salad.

---

    9 ounces fresh or 6 ounces dry
         fettuccine, cut or broken in rough
         ¼-inch "squares" (about 2 cups
         fresh, 1 cup dry)
   12 ounces fresh spinach, thick stems
         removed (about 5 packed cups),
         cooked, drained and squeezed dry
   ¾ cup beef broth
    1 tablespoon butter or margarine
    2 ounces thinly sliced prosciutto or
         Canadian bacon, cut in thin
         1½-inch-long strips (about ⅔ cup)
   ⅔ cup grated Parmesan cheese
   ¼ teaspoon pepper
  Salt (optional)

1. Bring a large pot of water to a boil over high heat. Add fettuccine and cook according to package directions (watch carefully; small pieces of pasta will cook quickly), stirring frequently, until firm to the bite. Drain in a colander.

2. Meanwhile, put spinach and beef broth in a food processor or blender and process until smooth.

3. Melt butter in a medium-size heavy saucepan over medium heat. Add prosciutto and cook about 2 minutes, stirring twice, until frizzled. Stir in spinach mixture, cheese and pepper. Taste and, if necessary, season with salt.

4. Add fettuccine and cook about 1 minute, until well blended and hot. Spoon into soup plates and serve.

Makes 2 main-dish or 4 appetizer servings. Per main-dish serving (with fresh pasta): 792 calories, 39 grams protein, 97 grams carbohydrate, 28 grams fat, 194 milligrams cholesterol with butter, 176 milligrams cholesterol with margarine, 944 milligrams sodium

Quadrettini

Macaroni with Beans

This hearty well-seasoned dish is most welcome on a cold winter night. Serve with garlic bread or crisp rolls. To remove seeds from peeled tomatoes, quarter them, then scoop out seeds with your fingers or a teaspoon.

¼ cup olive oil
5 slices bacon (about 4 ounces), cut in
    1-inch pieces
2 large onions, chopped
2 medium-size carrots, chopped
1 cup plus 2 tablespoons minced
    fresh parsley
2 tablespoons dried basil leaves
1 teaspoon dried oregano leaves
1 can (16 ounces) tomatoes, drained,
    or 4 small fresh tomatoes, peeled
    (see Peeling Tomatoes, page 10),
    seeded and chopped
2 cups cooked white beans (pea, navy
    or Great Northern) or 1 can
    (16 ounces) white beans (navy or
    cannellini), drained (reserve ½ cup
    cooking liquid or liquid from can)
2 teaspoons salt
1 teaspoon pepper, or to taste
1 pound elbow macaroni
¼ cup butter or margarine, at room
    temperature
½ cup grated Parmesan or other sharp
    cheese, plus additional grated
    cheese to taste

1. Heat oil in a Dutch oven over medium heat. Add bacon and cook until about halfway crisp. Stir in onions, carrots, 1 cup of the parsley, the basil and oregano and cook until vegetables are wilted.

2. Add tomatoes, reserved bean liquid, salt and pepper. Raise heat to high and bring to a boil. Reduce heat to low. Cover and simmer about 10 minutes, until vegetables are tender.

3. Add drained beans and simmer 20 minutes longer.

4. Meanwhile, bring a large pot of water to a boil over high heat. Add macaroni and cook according to package directions, stirring frequently, until firm to the bite. Drain in a colander.

5. Transfer macaroni to a large bowl. Toss macaroni with bits of the butter and ½ cup of the Parmesan. Pour vegetable mixture over pasta and toss to mix. Spoon into bowls. Sprinkle more cheese and remaining 2 tablespoons parsley over top and serve immediately.

Makes 8 servings. Per serving (with Parmesan cheese): 666 calories, 25 grams protein, 87 grams carbohydrate, 25 grams fat, 33 milligrams cholesterol with butter, 15 milligrams cholesterol with margarine, 841 milligrams sodium

Fettuccine with Prosciutto, Peas and Peppers

A classic recipe guaranteed to become a family favorite.

12 ounces fettuccine
¼ cup butter or margarine
4 ounces prosciutto or fully cooked
    ham, cut in julienne strips
1 cup frozen tiny peas
½ cup roasted red peppers (from a jar),
    cut in julienne strips
1 cup heavy cream
Pepper to taste
½ cup grated Parmesan cheese

1. Bring a large pot of water to a boil over high heat. Add fettuccine and cook according to package directions, stirring frequently, until firm to the bite. Drain in a colander.

2. Meanwhile, melt butter in a large skillet over medium heat. Add prosciutto and cook 1 minute. Add peas and roasted peppers and cook 1 minute longer.

3. Stir cream and pepper into skillet. Reduce heat to low and cook, stirring constantly, until slightly thickened.

4. Transfer fettuccine to a large heated serving bowl. Add sauce and Parmesan and toss to coat. Serve immediately.

Makes 4 servings. Per serving: 797 calories, 24 grams protein, 70 grams carbohydrate, 47 grams fat, 224 milligrams cholesterol with butter, 188 milligrams cholesterol with margarine, 547 milligrams sodium

---

Prosciutto

Prosciutto, Italian ham, is produced in the United States and in Italy. It is ham that has been seasoned, salt-cured (but not smoked) and air-dried. If possible, buy prosciutto at an Italian specialty store. Make sure it is well trimmed and sliced as thinly as possible or it will be tough. Use prosciutto sparingly, as it is expensive and has a strong (but delicious) salty flavor. A little is all you need to flavor a dish.

Spaghetti with Spinach and Bacon

The creamed spinach and milk make the sauce.

1 pound spaghetti
1 package (9 ounces) frozen creamed
    spinach, thawed
¾ cup milk
Pepper to taste
2 tablespoons vegetable oil, butter or
    margarine
1 clove garlic, minced
8 ounces bacon, crisply cooked,
    drained and crumbled
⅓ cup grated Parmesan cheese

1. Bring a large pot of water to a boil over high heat. Add spaghetti and cook according to package directions, stirring frequently, until firm to the bite. Drain in a colander.

2. Meanwhile, put spinach, milk and pepper in a medium-size saucepan. Cook over medium heat, stirring occasionally, until heated through and well blended. Remove from heat. Cover and keep warm.

3. Heat oil in spaghetti cooking pot over medium heat. Add garlic and cook about 1 minute, stirring constantly, until fragrant. Add spaghetti and toss. Add spinach mixture to spaghetti and toss lightly until well coated and hot.

4. Transfer to a large heated serving bowl. Sprinkle with bacon and Parmesan and serve.

Makes 4 servings. Per serving (with oil): 679 calories, 25 grams protein, 94 grams carbohydrate, 22 grams fat, 27 milligrams cholesterol, 450 milligrams sodium

Fettuccine con Ceci

You can also make this with any canned beans you happen to have on hand.

12 ounces fettuccine
4 slices bacon, cut up
1 clove garlic, minced
¼ cup vegetable oil
1 can (19 ounces) chick-peas,
    drained, liquid reserved
1 jar (7 ounces) roasted red peppers,
    drained, cut in strips
2 tablespoons chopped fresh parsley
½ teaspoon dried rosemary leaves,
    crumbled
⅛ teaspoon crushed red-pepper flakes
12 pitted large ripe olives, quartered
½ teaspoon salt

1. Bring a large pot of water to a boil over high heat. Add fettuccine and cook according to package directions, stirring frequently, until firm to the bite. Drain in a colander.

2. Meanwhile, cook bacon and garlic in oil in a medium-size skillet over medium-high heat 5 minutes, stirring frequently, until bacon is lightly browned.

3. Stir chick-peas, roasted peppers, parsley, rosemary and crushed red pepper into skillet and cook 5 minutes longer, stirring occasionally.

4. Stir in olives, salt and reserved chick-pea liquid. Simmer 5 minutes, until liquid is reduced by half.

5. Transfer fettuccine to a large heated serving bowl. Pour sauce over fettuccine. Toss to coat and serve.

Makes 4 servings. Per serving: 670 calories, 20 grams protein, 89 grams carbohydrate, 26 grams fat, 88 milligrams cholesterol, 456 milligrams sodium

Sausage

Pasta with Italian-Sausage Sauce

Make a spinach or escarole salad with Italian dressing to serve alongside.

1 teaspoon salt
8 ounces capellini (angel-hair pasta)
1 teaspoon plus 1 tablespoon olive oil
1 pound hot or sweet Italian sausage, removed from casings
2 medium-size zucchini (about 6 ounces each), quartered lengthwise, then thinly sliced crosswise
½ cup frozen or fresh chopped onion
1 jar (about 32 ounces) marinara sauce

1. Bring a large pot of water to a boil over high heat. Stir in salt, then capellini and cook according to package directions, stirring frequently, until firm to the bite. Drain in a colander. Transfer to a large heated serving bowl. Toss with 1 teaspoon of the oil to prevent sticking and cover to keep warm.

2. Meanwhile, heat remaining 1 tablespoon oil in a large skillet, preferably nonstick, over medium-high heat. Crumble in sausage and cook 4 to 5 minutes, stirring to break up any large chunks, until browned.

3. Stir in zucchini and onion. Cover and cook 3 minutes, stirring occasionally, until zucchini is crisp-tender. Add marinara sauce and bring to a boil.

4. Pour sauce over pasta in serving bowl. Toss well to coat and serve.

Makes 4 servings. Per serving: 814 calories, 28 grams protein, 70 grams carbohydrate, 49 grams fat, 86 milligrams cholesterol, 2,264 milligrams sodium

Pasta with Italian-Sausage Sauce

Sausage-and-Peppers Pasta Sauce

This recipe makes 18 cups of sauce, so freeze the extra in meal-size portions. Tip: Cool sauce completely and spoon into zipper-closure freezer bags. Freeze flat and when frozen, stack the bags. Allow 1 cupful per person plus 3 to 4 ounces freshly cooked spaghetti or linguine.

- 2 pounds sweet Italian sausage, removed from casings
- 1 pound ground turkey
- ¼ cup olive oil
- 1½ cups finely chopped onions
- 1 tablespoon minced fresh garlic
- 3 medium-size green and/or red bell peppers, cut in ¼-inch-wide strips
- 1¼ pounds zucchini, cut in ⅛-inch-thick rounds
- 1 pound mushrooms, thinly sliced
- 4 cans (28 ounces each) crushed tomatoes
- 1 tablespoon dried basil leaves
- 1 teaspoon dried marjoram leaves

1. Crumble sausage meat into a Dutch oven. Cook over medium-high heat about 15 minutes, stirring two or three times to break up large chunks, until sausage is browned. Remove to a bowl with a slotted spoon. Drain all but 2 tablespoons drippings from pot.

2. Add ground turkey to Dutch oven and cook about 10 minutes, stirring twice, until no longer pink. Remove to bowl with sausage.

3. Add oil to Dutch oven and heat. Stir in onions, garlic, bell peppers, zucchini and mushrooms. Cook about 15 minutes, stirring two or three times, until peppers are nearly tender.

4. Stir tomatoes, herbs, cooked sausage and turkey into vegetables. Bring to a boil. Reduce heat to medium-low, cover and simmer 15 minutes. Uncover and simmer 45 minutes longer, stirring occasionally, until vegetables are tender and sauce is thick. Use at once or cool completely. Pack, label and freeze up to three months.

Makes 18 cups. Per cup: 270 calories, 16 grams protein, 13 grams carbohydrate, 16 grams fat, 37 milligrams cholesterol, 538 milligrams sodium

Pepperoni Pasta

Pepperoni is usually found gracing pizzas, but it's good in pasta sauce, too.

- 1 pound spaghetti
- 3 tablespoons vegetable oil
- 1 large onion, sliced
- 2 large cloves garlic, halved
- 4 ounces sliced pepperoni
- 1 can (15 ounces) tomato sauce
- 2 large roasted peppers (from a jar), cut in strips
- 1 teaspoon dried basil leaves
- 1 teaspoon dried oregano leaves

1. Bring a large pot of water to a boil over high heat. Add spaghetti and cook according to package directions, stirring frequently, until firm to the bite. Drain in a colander.

2. Meanwhile, heat oil in a large skillet over medium-high heat. Add onion and garlic and cook until golden, stirring occasionally. Discard garlic.

3. Add pepperoni to skillet and cook 2 minutes, stirring frequently. Add tomato sauce, roasted peppers and herbs. Simmer 5 minutes to blend flavors.

4. Transfer spaghetti to a large heated serving bowl. Pour sauce over spaghetti; toss to coat well and serve.

Makes 4 servings. Per serving: 710 calories, 23 grams protein, 99 grams carbohydrate, 25 grams fat, 22 milligrams cholesterol, 1,238 milligrams sodium

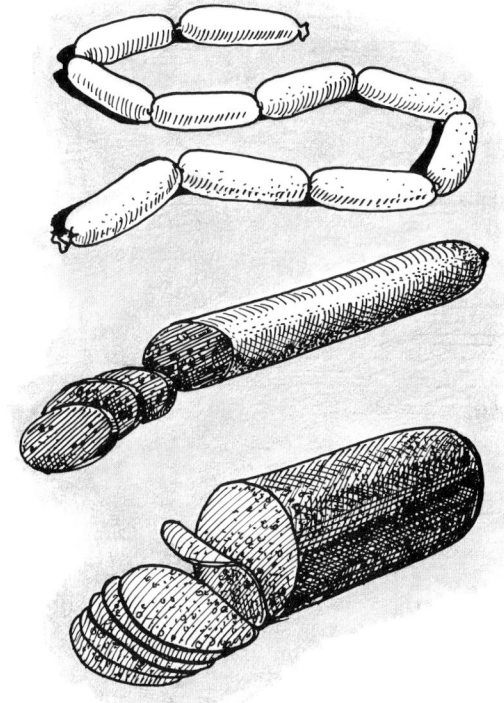

Sausage-and-Peppers Pasta Sauce

Pasta
with Seafood

*Two of America's healthful favorites,
pasta and seafood, come together in these dishes
featuring shrimp, clams or fish.*

Fettuccine with Salmon Sauce

Fish

Fettuccine with Salmon Sauce

Serve with a big salad and crusty bread.

- 12 ounces fettuccine
- 3 tablespoons butter or margarine
- 3 tablespoons all-purpose flour
- 2 cups milk
- 1 tablespoon Dijon mustard
- ¼ teaspoon salt
- ¼ teaspoon ground red pepper
- 1 package (10 ounces) frozen chopped spinach
- 1 can (15½ ounces) red or pink salmon, drained

For garnish: snipped fresh dill

1. Bring a large pot of water to a boil over high heat. Add fettuccine and cook according to package directions, stirring frequently, until firm to the bite. Drain in a colander.

2. Meanwhile, melt butter in a medium-size saucepan over medium heat. Add flour and cook 2 to 3 minutes, stirring constantly, until smooth and frothy. Add milk, mustard, salt and pepper and stir until smooth.

3. Add spinach to sauce and bring to a simmer, stirring occasionally to break up spinach. Cook 6 to 8 minutes, until sauce is thickened and smooth.

4. Add salmon to hot spinach sauce and stir to break up large chunks. Remove from heat.

5. Transfer fettuccine to a large heated platter or bowl. Pour sauce over pasta and toss to mix well. Sprinkle with dill and serve.

Makes 4 servings. Per serving: 646 calories, 38 grams protein, 74 grams carbohydrate, 22 grams fat, 157 milligrams cholesterol, 910 milligrams sodium

Spinach Pasta with Dilled Salmon Sauce

The salmon sauce is good on any pasta.

- 12 ounces spinach fettuccine or linguine, preferably fresh
- 1½ cups frozen green peas
- 4 tablespoons butter or margarine
- 1 cup half-and-half
- ½ cup freshly grated Parmesan cheese (2 ounces)
- 2 tablespoons chopped fresh dill or parsley
- 1 can (15½ ounces) salmon, drained and flaked

Pepper to taste

1. Bring a large pot of water to a boil over high heat. Add fresh pasta and peas and cook 5 minutes, stirring frequently, until pasta is firm to the bite and peas are tender. (If using dry pasta, add peas during last 3 minutes of cooking.) Drain in a colander.

2. Quickly melt butter in the pasta cooking pot. Stir in half-and-half, Parmesan and dill. Stir over medium-low heat 2 minutes, until cheese melts.

3. Stir in pasta, peas and salmon. Toss gently to coat thoroughly with sauce. Serve immediately in soup plates. Season with pepper.

Makes 4 servings. Per serving (with fettuccine): 833 calories, 45 grams protein, 72 grams carbohydrate, 40 grams fat, 198 milligrams cholesterol with butter, 162 milligrams cholesterol with margarine, 419 milligrams sodium

Butterflies with Salmon and Spinach

★ SPECIAL—AND WORTH IT

Butterflies with Salmon and Spinach

Chef Joyce Goldstein, owner of Square One restaurant in San Francisco, created this fast, light and pretty dish. The sauce takes only 6 minutes to prepare.

12 ounces farfalle pasta (butterflies, bow ties)
 1 cup heavy cream
 1 tablespoon grated fresh lemon peel
 2 tablespoons lemon juice
 1 teaspoon salt
 ¼ teaspoon pepper
 1 pound spinach, thick stems removed and leaves cut in fine shreds (about 6 loosely packed cups)
 1 pound boned and skinned raw salmon, cut in 1-inch cubes
For garnish: 2 tablespoons toasted pignoli (pine nuts, see Pignoli, page 21)

1. Bring a large pot of water to a boil over high heat. Add farfalle and cook according to package directions, stirring frequently, until firm to the bite. Drain in a colander.

2. Mix cream, lemon peel, juice, salt and pepper in a large skillet. Bring to a simmer over medium heat. Add spinach and cook about 1 minute, stirring constantly, just until wilted.

3. Add salmon to skillet. Cook about 2 minutes, gently turning pieces in sauce just until salmon is opaque in the center. Do not overcook.

4. Transfer pasta to a large heated serving bowl. Pour sauce over pasta and toss gently to mix. Sprinkle with pignoli and serve immediately.

Makes 4 servings. Per serving (without pignoli): 769 calories, 34 grams protein, 70 grams carbohydrate, 40 grams fat, 114 milligrams cholesterol, 658 milligrams sodium

Swordfish-Olive Pasta

Serve this over twists, shells or ridged ziti to catch all the tangy bits of olive and capers. This dish makes two hearty main-course servings or four first-course servings.

  8 ounces swordfish without skin, about ¾ inch thick
  8 ounces pasta, your choice
  ¼ cup olive oil
  ½ cup thinly sliced onion
  2 large cloves garlic, minced
  1 tablespoon drained capers
  1 teaspoon dried oregano leaves
  ¾ cup finely chopped pitted Greek-style olives

1. Turn on broiler. Line a broiler-pan rack with foil. Put swordfish on rack and broil about 4 inches from heat source 8 minutes. Turn and broil 3 minutes longer, until fish is just cooked through in the center. Transfer fish to a cutting board. Cover loosely with foil to keep warm.

2. Meanwhile, bring a medium-size pot of water to a boil over high heat. Add pasta and cook according to package directions, stirring frequently, until firm to the bite. Drain in a colander.

3. Heat oil in a small skillet over medium-high heat. Add onion and garlic and cook until tender. Stir in capers and oregano and remove from heat.

4. Transfer pasta to a medium-size heated serving bowl. Cut fish in thin strips. Place fish, olives and onion-caper mixture over hot pasta and toss gently. Serve immediately.

Makes 2 main-dish servings or 4 first-course servings. Per main-dish serving: 891 calories, 36 grams protein, 92 grams carbohydrate, 42 grams fat, 57 milligrams cholesterol, 971 milligrams sodium

Ziti with Tuna and Fresh Tomato Sauce

For a change, sprinkle this pasta dish with a little vinegar and serve it chilled.

  8 ounces ziti
  1 pound ripe fresh tomatoes, cut in ½-inch chunks (about 2 cups)
  8 ounces zucchini, quartered lengthwise, then cut crosswise in ½-inch pieces (about 1½ cups)
  1 can (12½ ounces) water-packed chunk light tuna, drained
  1 medium-size red onion, finely chopped (about ½ cup)
  ½ cup olive oil
  ½ cup pitted ripe olives, chopped
  ⅓ cup chopped fresh basil leaves or 2 tablespoons dried basil, crumbled
  1 teaspoon dried oregano leaves, crumbled
  ½ teaspoon salt
  ¼ teaspoon crushed red-pepper flakes
Grated Parmesan cheese (optional)

1. Bring a medium-size pot of water to a boil over high heat. Add ziti and cook according to package directions, stirring frequently, until firm to the bite. Drain in a colander.

2. Mix tomatoes, zucchini, tuna, onion, oil, olives, basil, oregano, salt and crushed red pepper in a large bowl until blended. Add hot ziti and toss to coat. Sprinkle with Parmesan cheese, if desired, and serve.

Makes 4 servings. Per serving (without Parmesan): 604 calories, 30 grams protein, 52 grams carbohydrate, 31 grams fat, 46 milligrams cholesterol, 441 milligrams sodium

Shells and Tuna Sauce

This is a winter favorite all over Italy, says Florence-born cooking teacher and writer Giuliano Bugialli. Serve as a light main dish with a salad and a loaf of crusty bread or as the first course of a hearty supper.

¼ cup olive oil
1 small red onion, finely chopped
    (about ⅓ cup)
1 can (14½ ounces) tomatoes,
    well drained
1 can (3½ ounces) olive oil-packed
    tuna, drained
½ teaspoon salt
¼ teaspoon pepper
8 ounces medium-size pasta shells

1. Heat oil in a medium-size heavy saucepan over low heat. Add onion and cook about 10 minutes, stirring occasionally, until golden brown.

2. Add tomatoes; break up with a fork and cook about 10 minutes, stirring occasionally, until liquid has evaporated. Add tuna and stir with a fork to break up chunks and mix well. Add salt and pepper and simmer 8 to 10 minutes.

3. Meanwhile, bring a large pot of water to a boil over high heat. Add pasta shells and cook according to package directions, stirring frequently, until firm to the bite. Drain in a colander.

4. Transfer shells to a medium-size heated serving bowl. Pour sauce over pasta; toss and serve.

Makes 4 servings. Per serving: 397 calories, 14 grams protein, 48 grams carbohydrate, 16 grams fat, 14 milligrams cholesterol, 571 milligrams sodium

Capellini with Tuna, Capers and Olives

Capellini with Tuna, Capers and Olives

1 teaspoon salt
12 ounces capellini (angel-hair pasta)
1 teaspoon plus 2 tablespoons
    olive oil
1 can (6½ ounces) oil-packed tuna, drained
4 canned anchovy fillets, minced, or 2
    teaspoons anchovy paste (optional)
½ cup pitted ripe olives
2 teaspoons drained capers
2 teaspoons minced fresh garlic
½ teaspoon dried basil leaves
1 can (28 ounces) Italian-style plum
    tomatoes, broken up

1. Bring a large pot of water to a boil over high heat. Add salt, then capellini and cook according to package directions, stirring frequently, until firm to the bite. Drain in a colander and toss with 1 teaspoon of the oil to prevent sticking.

2. Meanwhile, heat remaining 2 tablespoons oil in a large skillet over high heat. Add tuna, anchovies, if desired, olives, capers, if desired, garlic and basil. Cook about 1 minute, stirring gently, until blended and heated through. Stir in tomatoes and bring to a boil. Simmer 4 to 5 minutes, until sauce thickens slightly.

3. Transfer capellini to a large heated serving bowl. Pour sauce over pasta; toss and serve.

Makes 4 servings. Per serving (with anchovies): 524 calories, 25 grams protein, 73 grams carbohydrate, 14 grams fat, 28 milligrams cholesterol, 777 milligrams sodium

Pasta with Tuna and Peas

Pasta with Tuna and Peas

A calorie-conscious dish because it's made with less fat, evaporated skimmed milk instead of whole milk, pasta instead of egg noodles plus water-packed tuna.

6 ounces spaghetti or other pasta
1 cup frozen green peas
2 teaspoons margarine
6 ounces mushrooms, sliced (about 3 cups)
¼ cup finely chopped celery
¼ cup finely chopped onion
2 tablespoons all-purpose flour
1 cup evaporated skimmed milk
1 cup chicken broth
½ teaspoon dried tarragon leaves
½ teaspoon salt
⅛ teaspoon pepper
1 can (about 13 ounces) water-packed tuna, drained and broken up
1 tablespoon grated Parmesan cheese

1. Bring a large pot of water to a boil over high heat. Add spaghetti and cook according to package directions, stirring frequently, until firm to the bite. About 2 minutes before pasta is done, add peas to pot. Drain peas and pasta in a colander.

2. Melt margarine in a medium-size nonstick saucepan over medium heat. Add mushrooms, celery and onion and cook about 3 minutes, until mushrooms start to release their liquid.

3. Sprinkle mushrooms with flour and cook 1 minute, stirring constantly. Stir in milk, broth, tarragon, salt and pepper. Cook 5 to 7 minutes, stirring constantly, until sauce is thickened and smooth.

4. Transfer spaghetti to a large heated serving bowl and toss with tuna. Pour sauce over pasta and toss to coat. Sprinkle with Parmesan and serve.

Makes 4 servings. Per serving: 409 calories, 41 grams protein, 57 grams carbohydrate, 4 grams fat, 65 milligrams cholesterol, 607 milligrams sodium

Shellfish

Shrimp, Orzo and Zucchini

Orzo is pasta that looks like rice.

  2 cups chicken broth
  1 cup chopped fresh or drained
    canned tomatoes
 12 ounces zucchini, thinly sliced
  1 cup orzo
  1 pound frozen shelled and
    deveined shrimp
 ⅓ cup loosely packed fresh basil
    leaves, chopped, or 2 teaspoons
    dried basil
  1 teaspoon salt
 ¼ teaspoon pepper
  1 cup crumbled feta cheese (4 ounces)

1. Mix broth, tomatoes and zucchini in a large skillet. Bring to a boil over high heat.

2. Add orzo and simmer 6 minutes, stirring occasionally.

3. Add shrimp, basil, salt and pepper. Reduce heat to medium. Simmer 5 minutes, stirring occasionally, until shrimp turn pink, orzo is tender and liquid is absorbed. Stir in feta and heat only until cheese is partially melted. Pour into a heated serving bowl and serve.

Makes 4 servings. Per serving: 423 calories, 35 grams protein, 50 grams carbohydrate, 8 grams fat, 211 milligrams cholesterol, 1,372 milligrams sodium

★ SPECIAL—AND WORTH IT
Tequila Shrimp with Angel-Hair Pasta

This recipe comes from Carroll O'Connor's (a.k.a. Archie Bunker) restaurant in Beverly Hills, California.

  5 large fresh tomatoes, finely
    chopped (about 4 cups)
 1¼ cups loosely packed fresh cilantro
    leaves, chopped
 ½ cup chopped onion
 1½ tablespoons finely chopped seeded
    fresh or canned jalapeño pepper
  1 teaspoon salt
 ¼ teaspoon pepper
  1 pound angel-hair pasta (capellini)
 ¼ cup olive oil
  1 pound medium-size shrimp
    (about 36), peeled (tails left on)
    and deveined
 ½ cup tequila
  2 teaspoons minced fresh garlic
For garnish: fresh cilantro leaves

1. Mix tomatoes, cilantro, onion, jalapeño pepper, salt and pepper in a medium-size bowl.

2. Bring a large pot of water to a boil over high heat. Add angel-hair pasta and cook according to package directions, stirring frequently, until firm to the bite. Drain in a colander.

3. Heat oil in a large deep nonstick skillet over high heat. Add shrimp and stir-fry 3 minutes, just until pink.

4. Add tequila and garlic to shrimp and stir-fry 1 minute. Add tomato mixture and stir-fry 15 to 20 seconds, just until hot.

5. Arrange pasta on plates or a large heated platter. Spoon shrimp mixture over pasta. Garnish with cilantro leaves and serve immediately.

Makes 6 servings. Per serving: 454 calories, 23 grams protein, 64 grams carbohydrate, 11 grams fat, 93 milligrams cholesterol, 470 milligrams sodium

Linguine with Shrimp and Green Peas

A salad of thinly sliced cucumbers, red onions and bell peppers dressed with sour cream and vinegar, and a good seeded Italian bread make a meal of this easy dish.

- 1 pound linguine
- 1 tablespoon olive or vegetable oil
- 1 box (10 ounces) frozen green peas
- ½ cup frozen or fresh chopped onion
- ½ cup frozen or fresh chopped green bell pepper
- 1 jar (about 32 ounces) plain spaghetti sauce
- 12 ounces frozen cooked peeled shrimp
- ½ teaspoon crushed red-pepper flakes

1. Bring a large pot of water to a boil over high heat. Add linguine and cook according to package directions, stirring frequently, until firm to the bite. Drain in a colander.

2. Meanwhile, heat oil in a Dutch oven over medium-high heat. Add peas, onion and bell pepper. Cook 3 to 5 minutes, stirring frequently, until vegetables are thawed or fresh vegetables tender.

3. Stir in spaghetti sauce, frozen shrimp and crushed red pepper. Bring to a boil. Reduce heat to medium-low. Cover and simmer 3 to 4 minutes, stirring once, until shrimp and vegetables are hot.

4. Transfer linguine to a large heated serving bowl. Spoon sauce over pasta. Toss to coat well and serve.

Makes 4 servings, 6 cups sauce. Per serving: 771 calories, 37 grams protein, 129 grams carbohydrate, 11 grams fat, 111 milligrams cholesterol, 1,736 milligrams sodium

Capellini with Double Clam Sauce

Capellini with Double Clam Sauce

On the side: a spinach salad with fresh mushrooms drizzled with Italian dressing.

- 6 ounces capellini (angel-hair pasta), broken in thirds
- 1 can (10 ounces) whole baby clams, undrained
- 1 can (10½ ounces) white clam sauce
- 1 bottle (8 ounces) clam juice
- ¾ cup water
- 1 tablespoon vegetable oil
- 1 medium-size ripe fresh tomato, cut in chunks
- ½ cup sliced green onions
- ¼ teaspoon crushed red-pepper flakes, or to taste

1. Put capellini in a large skillet. Drain juices from cans of clams and clam sauce into skillet. Add bottled clam juice, ½ cup of the water and the oil. Cover and bring to a boil over high heat. Boil 3 minutes, stirring three times with a fork to separate strands of pasta.

2. Add whole clams, drained clam sauce, tomato, green onions and crushed red pepper. Reduce heat to low. Cover and simmer 3 minutes, until heated through and pasta is tender. Stir in remaining ¼ cup water.

3. Remove from heat. Transfer to a medium-size heated serving bowl and serve immediately.

Makes 4 servings. Per serving: 315 calories, 17 grams protein, 42 grams carbohydrate, 10 grams fat, 38 milligrams cholesterol, 840 milligrams sodium

Linguine with Red Clam Sauce

Linguine is the classic pasta for clam sauce. Serve as a first course or double the recipe to serve four as a main course.

    9 ounces fresh or 6 ounces
          dry linguine
    2 tablespoons olive oil
 1½ teaspoons minced fresh garlic
    ⅓ cup dry white wine (see Notes)
    1 jar (about 15 ounces)
          marinara sauce
    1 tablespoon tomato paste
  12 fresh cherrystone clams, shucked
          and coarsely chopped (about ¾
          cup; see Notes), juices reserved,
          or 1 can (10½ ounces) chopped
          clams, drained and juices
          reserved
    2 tablespoons chopped fresh parsley
    1 tablespoon butter or margarine
    ¼ teaspoon pepper, or to taste
Salt (optional)

1. Bring a large pot of water to a boil over high heat. Add linguine and cook according to package directions, stirring frequently, until firm to the bite. Drain in a colander.

2. Heat oil in a medium-size saucepan over medium heat. Add garlic and cook 2 to 3 minutes, stirring frequently, until golden. Add wine and bring to a boil. Stir in marinara sauce, tomato paste and reserved clam juice. Return to a boil. Reduce heat to low. Add clams and simmer 5 minutes to develop flavor and heat clams. Remove from heat.

3. Stir parsley, butter and pepper into sauce. Taste and, if necessary, season with salt and additional pepper.

4. Transfer linguine to a heated serving bowl. Pour sauce over linguine; toss to mix and serve immediately.

Makes 2 main-dish or 4 appetizer servings. Per main-dish serving (with fresh pasta): 979 calories, 36 grams protein, 131 grams carbohydrate, 31 grams fat, 196 milligrams cholesterol with butter, 181 milligrams cholesterol with margarine, 2,121 milligrams sodium

Notes: You can omit the wine and add ½ teaspoon lemon juice with the clam juice.

If necessary, add water or bottled clam juice to reserved clam juice to measure at least ½ cup.

Pasta with Clam and Spinach Sauce

Good with a tomato-and-cucumber salad. Spinach can be thawed on the countertop, in the refrigerator overnight or in the microwave oven.

    1 teaspoon salt
  12 ounces capellini (angel-hair pasta)
    4 tablespoons olive oil
    2 teaspoons minced fresh garlic
    1 teaspoon dried oregano leaves
    ¼ teaspoon crushed red-pepper flakes
          (optional)
    2 cans (10 ounces each) whole baby
          clams, undrained
    1 box (10 ounces) frozen leaf spinach,
          thawed and squeezed dry

1. Bring a large pot of water to a boil over high heat. Stir in salt, then capellini and cook according to package directions, stirring frequently, until firm to the bite. Drain in a colander. Transfer to a large heated serving bowl. Toss with 1 tablespoon of the oil to prevent sticking and cover to keep warm.

2. Meanwhile, heat remaining 3 tablespoons oil in a large skillet over medium-high heat. Add garlic and cook 30 seconds, stirring constantly. Stir in oregano and crushed red pepper, if desired.

3. Drain liquid from clams into skillet and stir in spinach. Bring to a boil. Reduce heat to medium-low; cover and simmer 3 minutes. Add clams and stir 1 minute, until hot. Pour sauce over capellini. Toss and serve immediately.

Makes 4 servings. Per serving: 528 calories, 24 grams protein, 72 grams carbohydrate, 16 grams fat, 45 milligrams cholesterol, 1,136 milligrams sodium

Pasta with Clam and Spinach Sauce

Linguine with White Clam Sauce

A crisp green salad, bread and fresh fruit complete the meal.

12 ounces linguine
¼ cup butter or margarine
¾ cup chopped onion
1 teaspoon minced fresh garlic
½ cup chopped fresh parsley
1 teaspoon dried basil leaves
½ teaspoon salt
Pepper to taste
2 cans (6½ ounces each) minced clams, undrained

1. Bring a large pot of water to a boil over high heat. Add linguine and cook according to package directions, stirring frequently, until firm to the bite. Drain in a colander.

2. Meanwhile, melt butter in a medium-size saucepan over medium heat. Add onion and garlic and cook about 5 minutes, stirring occasionally, until onion is tender.

3. Add parsley, basil, salt and pepper. Cook 3 to 4 minutes, stirring occasionally. Add clams and their liquid and cook 1 minute, just until hot.

4. Transfer linguine to a large heated serving bowl. Pour sauce over linguine; toss to coat well and serve.

Makes 4 servings. Per serving: 488 calories, 20 grams protein, 71 grams carbohydrate, 13 grams fat, 71 milligrams cholesterol with butter, 35 milligrams cholesterol with margarine, 1,042 milligrams sodium

★ SPECIAL—AND WORTH IT
Pasta with Seafood

Delicious served with a Boston lettuce, watercress and Belgian endive salad tossed with a light vinaigrette. For a special touch, grate fresh Parmesan cheese on the large holes of your grater to sprinkle over the salad.

1 pint medium-size shucked fresh oysters, drained (about 24)
12 ounces fettuccine
½ cup unsalted butter or margarine
¼ cup olive oil
1½ tablespoons minced fresh garlic
1 package (12 ounces) frozen shelled and deveined shrimp, thawed
1 package (6 ounces) frozen snow-crab meat, thawed
¾ cup chopped fresh Italian parsley
1 tablespoon lemon juice
½ teaspoon salt
¼ teaspoon pepper
⅛ teaspoon ground red pepper

1. Drop oysters into boiling water to cover in a medium-size saucepan. Remove from heat. Let stand uncovered 3 minutes. Drain and set aside.

2. Meanwhile, bring a large pot of water to a boil over high heat. Add fettuccine and cook according to package directions, stirring frequently, until firm to the bite. Drain in a colander.

3. Heat butter and oil in a large skillet over medium heat. Stir in garlic and cook 2 to 3 minutes, stirring frequently, until golden. Add shrimp and cook 2 minutes, stirring frequently.

4. Add crab meat, oysters, parsley, lemon juice, salt, pepper and ground red pepper to skillet. Stir gently to mix and cook just until hot.

5. Transfer pasta to a large heated serving bowl. Pour seafood mixture over pasta. Toss to mix and serve immediately.

Makes 4 servings. Per serving: 814 calories, 40 grams protein, 71 grams carbohydrate, 40 grams fat, 267 milligrams cholesterol with butter, 195 milligrams cholesterol with margarine, 531 milligrams sodium

Seafood and Pasta Marinara

Serve with grated Parmesan or shredded mozzarella cheese.

- 1 jar (about 16 ounces) marinara sauce
- 3½ cups water
- ½ teaspoon salt
- 8 ounces capellini (angel-hair pasta)
- 12 ounces imitation crabmeat chunks, no need to thaw if frozen
- 3 cups frozen cut broccoli (from a 20-ounce bag)
- 1 teaspoon dried oregano leaves

1. Bring marinara sauce, water and salt to a boil in a large skillet over high heat. Break capellini into fourths and add to skillet. Return to a boil and reduce heat to low. Cover and simmer about 4 minutes, stirring often, until pasta is almost tender.

2. Meanwhile, separate frozen crabmeat chunks. Add to skillet along with broccoli and oregano. Raise heat to medium-high and return to a boil. Reduce heat to low. Cover and simmer about 3 minutes, stirring frequently, until pasta and broccoli are tender and crabmeat is hot.

3. Transfer to a heated platter and serve.

Makes 4 servings. Per serving: 422 calories, 24 grams protein, 74 grams carbohydrate, 3 grams fat, 13 milligrams cholesterol, 1,870 milligrams sodium

Seafood and Pasta Marinara

Baked or Stuffed Pasta

With the warm glow of tomato sauce and lots of oozing cheese, lasagne, manicotti and baked ziti make especially satisfying meals. Also inviting are stuffed pillows or rings of pasta tossed with luscious sauces.

Microwave Lasagne with Meat Sauce

Lasagne

✳ MICROWAVE
Microwave Lasagne with Meat Sauce

Microwaves make short work of many traditional recipes, but that's not the only time-saver here. There is no need to cook the noodles. The sauce and cheeses provide enough moisture; tightly covering the baking dish retains that moisture, so the pasta cooks. The lasagne is "baked" on medium (rather than high) for most of the time.

1 **pound lean ground beef**
1 **medium-size onion, finely chopped (about ½ cup)**
2 **teaspoons minced fresh garlic**
2 **cans (15 ounces each) tomato sauce**
1 **teaspoon salt**
1 **teaspoon granulated sugar**
1 **teaspoon** *each* **dried basil and oregano leaves**
¼ **teaspoon pepper**
¼ **teaspoon crushed red-pepper flakes**
9 **lasagne noodles (about 7 ounces, uncooked)**
1 **container (15 ounces) ricotta cheese**
2 **cups shredded mozzarella cheese (8 ounces)**
1 **cup coarsely shredded Parmesan cheese (4 ounces)**

1. Crumble beef into a microwave-safe colander set in a deep 2-quart casserole. Add onion and garlic. Cover loosely with waxed paper.

2. Microwave on high 3 minutes. Stir to break up meat. Cover and microwave 2 to 3 minutes longer, until meat is no longer pink and onion is tender.

3. Discard drippings and put meat mixture in same casserole. Stir in tomato sauce, salt, sugar, herbs and peppers; cover with waxed paper.

4. Microwave on high 5 to 6 minutes, stirring once, until sauce is hot.

5. Spread 1 cup of the sauce in the bottom of a 12x8x2-inch microwave-safe baking dish. Top with 3 noodles in a single layer, 1 cup of the ricotta, ⅔ cup of the mozzarella, ⅓ cup of the Parmesan and 1½ cups of the sauce. Repeat with a second layer. Top with remaining noodles, then the remaining sauce, mozzarella and Parmesan.

6. Cover tightly with a lid or vented plastic wrap. Microwave on high 6 to 8 minutes. Rotate dish ½ turn. Reduce power to medium. Microwave 30 to 32 minutes, rotating dish ½ turn once, until noodles are tender.

7. Let lasagne stand covered 5 to 10 minutes to equalize temperature before serving. Cut into portions and serve.

Makes 8 servings. Per serving: 467 calories, 28 grams protein, 31 grams carbohydrate, 24 grams fat, 93 milligrams cholesterol, 1,380 milligrams sodium

Three-Cheese Lasagne

The sauce for this exceptional recipe can be made ahead and refrigerated up to three days or frozen.

Meat Sauce

2 tablespoons olive oil
½ cup finely chopped onion
2 teaspoons minced fresh garlic
1 pound lean ground beef
1 can (28 ounces) tomatoes, broken up
2 cups water
1 can (6 ounces) tomato paste
1 teaspoon salt
2 tablespoons minced fresh basil leaves or 2 teaspoons dried basil, crumbled
1 teaspoon granulated sugar
One 2-inch-long bay leaf
½ teaspoon pepper

Noodles and Filling

9 lasagne noodles (about 8 ounces)
1 container (15 ounces) ricotta cheese
2 cups shredded mozzarella cheese (8 ounces)
½ cup grated Parmesan cheese

1. To make meat sauce: Heat oil in a Dutch oven over medium heat. Add onion and cook 5 minutes, stirring once or twice, until nearly tender. Add garlic and cook 1 minute. Crumble beef into pot and stir until no longer pink.

2. Stir in tomatoes, water, tomato paste, salt, basil, sugar, bay leaf and pepper. Raise heat to high and bring to a boil. Reduce heat to low and simmer 1½ hours, stirring every half hour, until sauce is thick. Remove from heat and discard bay leaf.

3. Heat oven to 325°F. Have ready a 13x9x1½-inch baking dish.

4. Bring a large pot of water to a boil over high heat. Add lasagne noodles and cook according to package directions, gently stirring a few times, until firm to the bite. Drain in a colander and rinse well under cold running water, being careful not to tear noodles. (If noodles start to stick, toss with a little olive oil.)

5. To assemble: Spread about 1 cup of the sauce in the bottom of baking dish. Top with 3 noodles in a single layer, another cup of the sauce, one third of the ricotta, one third of the mozzarella and one third of the Parmesan. Repeat layers twice, reserving about ¼ cup sauce, then spoon that over the top.

6. Bake 45 minutes, until hot and bubbly. Let stand 15 minutes before cutting and serving.

Makes 8 servings. Per serving: 546 calories, 30 grams protein, 34 grams carbohydrate, 32 grams fat, 123 milligrams cholesterol, 641 milligrams sodium

Microwave Method: Omit the oil in meat sauce and do not cook the noodles. Crumble beef into a microwave-safe colander set in a deep 2-quart casserole. Add onion and garlic. Cover loosely with waxed paper and microwave on high 3 minutes. Stir to break up meat. Cover and microwave on high 2 to 3 minutes longer, until meat is no longer pink. Discard the drippings and put meat in same casserole. Stir in remaining sauce ingredients. Cover with waxed paper and microwave on high 5 to 6 minutes, stirring once, until sauce is hot. Discard bay leaf. Assemble lasagne as directed above, using uncooked noodles. Cover tightly with a lid or vented plastic wrap. Microwave on high 6 to 8 minutes. Rotate casserole ½ turn. Reduce power to medium. Microwave 30 to 32 minutes, rotating casserole ½ turn once, until noodles are tender. Let stand covered 5 to 10 minutes to equalize temperature and make cutting easier.

Garden Lasagne

This recipe makes two lasagnes, one to serve right away and another to freeze (see Note). Line the pan of the lasagne to be frozen with heavy-duty foil, remove the frozen lasagne, stash it in the freezer and use the dish for something else.

1½ pounds lasagne noodles
  8 cups milk
  1 clove garlic, halved
  1 cup butter or margarine
  1 cup all-purpose flour
1¼ teaspoons salt
  ¼ teaspoon pepper
  ⅛ teaspoon ground nutmeg
  2 cups grated Parmesan cheese
  ¼ cup minced fresh parsley
  2 boxes (10 ounces each) frozen
      mixed vegetables, thawed and
      drained
  2 boxes (10 ounces each) frozen
      chopped broccoli, thawed and
      drained

Garden Lasagne

1. Bring a large pot of water to a boil over high heat. Add lasagne noodles and cook according to package directions, gently stirring a few times, until firm to the bite. Drain in a colander and rinse well with cold running water, being careful not to tear noodles. (If noodles start to stick, toss with a little olive oil.)

2. Heat milk with garlic in a large saucepan over medium heat until small bubbles appear around edges. Remove milk from heat; discard garlic.

3. Measure and set aside 2 tablespoons of the butter. Melt remaining butter in a Dutch oven over medium heat. Stir in flour, salt, pepper and nutmeg. Cook 2 minutes, stirring constantly, until bubbly. Stir in hot milk until smooth. Reduce heat to low and simmer about 10 minutes, stirring constantly, until thickened. Stir in 1⅓ cups of the Parmesan and the parsley.

4. Heat oven to 425°F. Lightly grease two shallow 3-quart baking dishes. (If freezing one of the lasagnes, line one dish with enough heavy-duty foil to bring up over and cover lasagne.)

5. Spread ⅓ cup of the sauce in each dish. Add vegetables to remaining sauce. Layer one fourth of the noodles and one fourth of the sauce mixture in each dish. Repeat layers, ending with sauce mixture. Sprinkle tops with remaining Parmesan and dot with the 2 tablespoons butter.

6. Bake 30 minutes or until browned and bubbly. Let stand 10 to 15 minutes before cutting and serving.

Makes two 3-quart casseroles, 8 servings each. Per serving: 455 calories, 17 grams protein, 49 grams carbohydrate, 21 grams fat, 104 milligrams cholesterol with butter, 68 milligrams cholesterol with margarine, 487 milligrams sodium

Note: To freeze, cool unbaked lasagne completely. Bring up foil to cover lasagne and freeze in baking dish. Remove from dish; wrap tightly. Return to freezer. To bake, remove from foil; place in baking dish. Partially thaw 2 hours at room temperature or in refrigerator overnight. Bake in 425°F oven 40 to 50 minutes, until browned and bubbly.

✴ MICROWAVE
Two-Meat Lasagne

Using part-skim cheeses and ground turkey instead of all beef helps reduce the fat in this lasagne. The lasagne noodles are baked uncooked.

Sauce
  1 pound ground turkey
  8 ounces lean ground beef
  3 cans (15 ounces each) tomato sauce
  1 can (16 ounces) tomatoes, broken up
1½ teaspoons Italian dried-herb seasoning
  1 teaspoon seasoned salt substitute
½ teaspoon minced fresh garlic
½ teaspoon pepper

Noodles and Filling
  2 containers (15 ounces each) part-skim ricotta cheese
  2 cups shredded part-skim mozzarella cheese (8 ounces)
  4 tablespoons grated Parmesan cheese
½ teaspoon pepper
  8 curly-edge lasagne noodles (about 8 ounces)

1. To make sauce: Crumble ground turkey and beef into a large deep skillet. Cook over medium-high heat about 10 minutes, stirring often to break up meat, until it loses its pink color.

2. Stir in tomato sauce, tomatoes, herb seasoning, salt substitute, garlic and pepper. Bring to a boil. Reduce heat to low and simmer 15 minutes, stirring three or four times. Remove from heat.

3. Heat oven to 375°F. Have a 13x9-inch baking pan ready.

4. Meanwhile, make filling: Mix ricotta, 1 cup of the mozzarella, 2 tablespoons of the Parmesan and the pepper in a medium-size bowl.

5. Spread 2 cups of the sauce in the bottom of baking pan. Top with 4 uncooked noodles slightly overlapping, half the cheese filling (about 2 cups) and half the remaining sauce (about 3 cups). Repeat with a second layer. Sprinkle remaining 1 cup mozzarella and 2 tablespoons Parmesan over top.

6. Bake 45 to 50 minutes, until noodles are tender and top is browned. Let stand 15 minutes before cutting and serving.

Makes 8 servings. Per serving: 575 calories, 41 grams protein, 41 grams carbohydrate, 28 grams fat, 120 milligrams cholesterol, 1,498 milligrams sodium

Microwave Method: For sauce, reduce Italian seasoning to 1 teaspoon and pepper to ¼ teaspoon. Crumble turkey and beef into a microwave-safe colander set in a 3-quart bowl. Or line a 3-quart bowl with a double thickness of paper towels and crumble turkey and beef on top of towels. Microwave on high 5 to 8 minutes, stirring twice, until meat is no longer pink. Pour off drippings or discard paper towels and put meat in same bowl. Stir in tomato sauce, tomatoes, herb seasoning, salt substitute, garlic and pepper. Microwave uncovered on high 12 to 16 minutes, until sauce is boiling. Cover with waxed paper. Let stand 5 minutes. Assemble as directed above in a 12x8x2-inch microwave-safe glass baking dish. Cover with a lid or vented plastic wrap. Microwave on high 6 minutes, rotating dish ½ turn after 3 minutes. Reduce power to medium. Microwave 28 to 30 minutes, rotating dish once, just until noodles are tender. Let stand covered 10 minutes.

Lasagne Marinara with Meat

A member of the onion family, shallots add a mild onion flavor to this lasagne. If shallots are not available, substitute the white part of green onions.

---

1 tablespoon olive oil
⅔ cup minced shallots (about 10 shallots)
3 cloves garlic, minced
8 ounces lean ground beef
1 pound fresh tomatoes, peeled (see Peeling Tomatoes, page 10) and chopped
1 tablespoon minced fresh parsley
¼ teaspoon granulated sugar (optional)
8 lasagne noodles (about 8 ounces)
1 cup part-skim ricotta cheese

1. Heat oil in a large skillet over medium heat. Add shallots and garlic and cook 1 minute. Crumble in ground beef and cook, breaking up large chunks with a spoon, until no longer pink.

2. Add tomatoes, parsley and sugar, if desired, and bring to a boil. Reduce heat to low. Cover and simmer 15 minutes.

3. Meanwhile, bring a large pot of water to a boil over high heat. Add lasagne noodles and cook according to package directions, gently stirring a few times, until firm to the bite. Drain in a colander and rinse well under cold running water, being careful not to tear noodles. (If noodles start to stick, toss with a little olive oil.)

4. Heat oven to 350°F. Grease an 11½x8½-inch baking dish.

5. Spread a thin layer of sauce in prepared baking dish. Layer half of the ricotta, one third of the remaining sauce, then half of the noodles. Repeat layers. Spoon remaining sauce over the top. Cover with foil and bake about 25 minutes, until hot and bubbly. Let stand 5 to 10 minutes before cutting and serving.

Makes 8 servings. Per serving: 247 calories, 13 grams protein, 27 grams carbohydrate, 10 grams fat, 56 milligrams cholesterol, 56 milligrams sodium

Olive Oil

☐ Olive oil is a natural partner to pasta. The distinctive, subtle flavor of the oil blends perfectly with the acidity of tomatoes and the nutty tang of Parmesan cheese. Whether used as an ingredient or as a tabletop condiment, olive oil will round out the flavors of a dish.

☐ Many studies have shown that it may lower the amounts of "bad" cholesterol in the blood since it is a monounsaturated oil.

☐ Supermarket shelves are well stocked with different types and grades of olive oil:

Pure: Most of our recipes were tested with pure olive oil. Because it has a mild flavor and a light golden color, it is the most suitable for cooking.

Virgin: This oil has a darker gold-to-green color and a stronger, more acidic, olive taste. It is best used in salads or sauces.

Extra Virgin: Made from the first pressing of the olives, this oil is the most expensive and has the most pronounced flavor and aroma. Save it for salads and cold sauces, or to drizzle over antipasto platters or sliced tomatoes.

Light: With a very delicate flavor and fragrance (but no fewer calories), light olive oil is suitable for all types of cooking and baking.

When stored properly, olive oil keeps longer than all other cooking oils. Store it in a cool cupboard in an airtight container protected from light for up to six months. Refrigeration is not necessary; it will not harm the oil, but it will make it thick and cloudy. To return the oil to a clear liquid state, simply leave it at room temperature.

Lasagne with Spinach and Italian Sausage

This makes two hefty dinners for four. After baking, refrigerate or freeze one lasagne for another day (see Note). This recipe calls for wide egg noodles instead of lasagne noodles.

Sauce
- 1 pound sweet Italian sausage, removed from casings
- 2 teaspoons minced fresh garlic
- 3 cans (16 ounces each) crushed tomatoes
- 1 cup water
- 2 teaspoons granulated sugar
- 1 teaspoon *each* dried basil and oregano leaves
- 1 large bay leaf
- ¼ teaspoon *each* salt and pepper

Spinach-Noodle Mixture
- 1 package (12 ounces) extra-wide curly egg noodles
- 4 large eggs
- 2 boxes (10 ounces each) frozen chopped spinach, thawed and squeezed dry
- 6 green onions, sliced
- 4 tablespoons grated Parmesan cheese
- ⅛ teaspoon ground nutmeg
- ⅛ teaspoon pepper

Topping
- 4 cups shredded mozzarella cheese (1 pound)
- 4 tablespoons grated Parmesan cheese

1. To make sauce: Crumble sausage into a Dutch oven. Cook over medium-high heat, breaking up pieces with a wooden spoon, until sausage is lightly browned. Drain off excess fat.

2. Stir remaining sauce ingredients into Dutch oven. Bring to a boil. Reduce heat to low and simmer uncovered 1 hour, stirring occasionally, until sauce is thick. Remove from heat. Discard bay leaf.

3. To make spinach-noodle mixture: Bring a large pot of water to a boil over high heat. Add noodles and cook 5 minutes, stirring frequently. Drain in a colander. Rinse under cold running water. Shake off excess water.

4. Beat eggs in a large bowl. Add noodles and remaining spinach-noodle-mixture ingredients. Mix gently, using hands or a large fork, until well blended.

5. Heat oven to 400°F. Grease two 9-inch square baking pans. (If freezing one lasagne, see Note.)

6. To assemble: Spread one quarter of the spinach-noodle mixture in each pan. Top each layer with one fourth of the sauce, then one fourth of the mozzarella. Repeat layers. Sprinkle 2 tablespoons of the Parmesan over each.

7. Bake both lasagnes 20 minutes, until hot and bubbly. Cool on a wire rack 15 minutes. Cut in squares and serve from pan.

Each pan makes 4 generous servings. Per serving: 571 calories, 30 grams protein, 44 grams carbohydrate, 31 grams fat, 179 milligrams cholesterol, 865 milligrams sodium

Note: If freezing lasagne, first line pan with enough heavy-duty foil to bring up over and cover lasagne. Assemble and bake as directed. Cool pan completely on rack. Wrap with foil, label and freeze. (After lasagne is frozen, it can be removed from the pan, if desired. Remove from foil and return to pan to defrost and heat.) To reheat, thaw in refrigerator overnight. Cover loosely with foil and bake in 325°F oven 20 minutes, until hot.

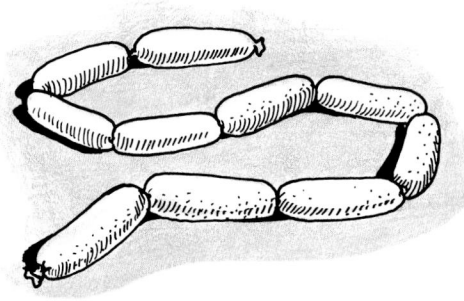

Hot from the Oven

⏱ MAKE-AHEAD
★ SPECIAL—AND WORTH IT
Pastitsio for a Party

This rich and full-flavored oven dish, a traditional Greek noodle pie with a ground-meat filling, is great for a large gathering. The meat sauce can be prepared ahead and refrigerated. Bake pastitsio at least 6 hours before serving so that it will cut neatly. Cool and refrigerate until ready to reheat and serve.

---

  1 cup plus 3 tablespoons butter or margarine
  1 cup finely chopped onion
  2 cloves garlic, minced
  2 pounds lean ground lamb
1½ pounds lean ground beef
  3 cups tomato sauce (homemade or bought)
  1 cup dry red wine
  ½ cup finely chopped fresh parsley
One 2-inch-long bay leaf
  1 teaspoon dried oregano leaves
  ½ teaspoon dried basil leaves
  ½ teaspoon ground cinnamon
1½ teaspoons salt, or to taste
  ½ teaspoon pepper, or to taste
  7 cups light cream or half-and-half
  2 cups milk
1½ cups all-purpose flour
Generous pinch ground nutmeg
Yolks from 10 large eggs
  2 cups ricotta cheese
1½ pounds elbow macaroni or ziti
1½ cups grated Romano cheese

1. Melt 3 tablespoons of the butter in a very large skillet or Dutch oven over medium heat. Add onion and cook, stirring frequently, until tender. Stir in garlic and cook 2 minutes, stirring frequently.

2. Raise heat to high. Crumble in lamb and beef and cook, breaking up pieces with a spoon, until browned. Add tomato sauce, wine, parsley, bay leaf, oregano, basil, cinnamon and ½ teaspoon *each* salt and pepper. Stir well and bring to a boil. Reduce heat to medium-low and cook sauce about 20 minutes, stirring frequently, until sauce is thickened. Remove from heat. Discard bay leaf and set sauce aside. (Sauce may be cooled and refrigerated up to two days at this point or frozen for longer storage. Thaw and heat before using.)

3. Heat 6 cups of the cream and the milk in a large saucepan over medium heat until bubbles appear around the edges. Remove from heat.

4. Melt remaining 1 cup butter in a large heavy nonaluminum saucepan or Dutch oven over medium heat. Stir in flour with a wire whisk or a wooden spoon until blended.

5. Gradually stir in hot cream-milk mixture, stirring constantly to prevent lumping. Bring sauce to a boil, stirring constantly. Reduce heat to low and simmer about 15 minutes, stirring very frequently, until sauce is thick and smooth. Season with remaining 1 teaspoon salt and the nutmeg. Remove from heat and let sauce cool 10 minutes.

6. Heat oven to 400°F. Grease a deep 7-quart baking pan or two 13x9-inch baking pans.

7. Beat egg yolks with remaining 1 cup cream in a large bowl. Gradually beat about 2 cups warm cream sauce into egg mixture. Scrape egg mixture into cream sauce and stir until blended. Beat in ricotta until well blended.

8. Spread half the uncooked macaroni in pan; sprinkle with half the Romano. Cover with half the cream-sauce mixture, smoothing sauce with the back of a large spoon. Spread on all of meat sauce. Top with layer of remaining macaroni, cream sauce and Romano.

9. Bake 55 minutes, until bubbly and covered with a golden-brown crust. Cool until warm on a wire rack and cover and refrigerate 6 hours, at least.

10. About 30 minutes before ready to serve, heat oven to 350°F. Cut pastitsio into serving portions. Cover pan with foil and bake 30 minutes, until heated through.

Makes 12 generous servings. Per serving (with light cream): 863 calories, 34 grams protein, 71 grams carbohydrate, 49 grams fat, 323 milligrams cholesterol with butter, 290 milligrams cholesterol with margarine, 1,121 milligrams sodium

Meatless Pastitsio

A simpler (and lower-calorie) version of the classic dish on the opposite page. For a change, make this with spinach, tomato or a whole-wheat pasta. Serve with a colorful salad of arugula, radicchio or red cabbage, Belgian endive and Boston lettuce. Toss the salad with a mustardy vinaigrette dressing and freshly made croutons. Since this is a hearty meal, add a simple dessert of cut-up ripe seasonal fruit sweetened with sugar or honey and store-bought macaroons.

 4 ounces ziti or other tubular
    macaroni
 2 cups spaghetti sauce (homemade
    or from a jar)
 6 large eggs
 1 cup plain yogurt
 ¼ cup grated Parmesan or
    Romano cheese
 ½ teaspoon salt
 ¼ teaspoon pepper

1. Heat oven to 400°F. Have ready a shallow medium-size baking dish.

2. Bring a medium-size pot of water to a boil over high heat. Add ziti and cook according to package directions, stirring frequently, until firm to the bite. Drain in a colander.

3. Spread spaghetti sauce in baking dish. Sprinkle ziti over sauce.

4. Beat eggs, yogurt, cheese, salt and pepper in a large bowl until well blended. Pour egg mixture over ziti.

5. Bake 25 to 30 minutes, until bubbly and egg mixture is set. Let stand 5 to 10 minutes before serving.

Makes 4 servings. Per serving: 342 calories, 21 grams protein, 34 grams carbohydrate, 13 grams fat, 340 milligrams cholesterol, 1,273 milligrams sodium

⏲ MAKE-AHEAD
✳ MICROWAVE
Baked Ziti with Spinach

This recipe makes enough for two pans of ziti, so it's perfect for a party. If a party is not in your plans, line one of the baking dishes with enough heavy-duty foil to bring up over and cover contents, assemble ziti and freeze unbaked. Remove from foil and return to baking pan to defrost and heat. Defrost in refrigerator overnight and bake uncovered at 400°F about 1 hour, until hot and bubbly.

24 ounces ziti (about 8 cups)
 2 jars (about 15 ounces each)
    marinara sauce
 2 cups shredded mozzarella cheese
    (8 ounces)
 2 boxes (9 ounces each) frozen
    creamed spinach, thawed
 2 tablespoons grated Parmesan
    cheese

1. Heat oven to 400°F. Lightly grease two 9-inch square baking dishes (or line one with heavy-duty foil as described above).

2. Bring a large pot of water to a boil over high heat. (If your pot isn't large enough, cook ziti in two batches. Remove first batch of ziti from water with a strainer. Return water to a boil and cook remaining pasta.) Add ziti and cook according to package directions, stirring frequently, until firm to the bite. Drain in a colander.

3. Return drained ziti to cooking pot. Stir in marinara sauce and mozzarella.

4. Spread 3 cups of the mixture in each baking dish. Top each with half the spinach and then half the remaining ziti mixture. Sprinkle each with 1 tablespoon of the Parmesan.

5. Bake ziti 15 to 20 minutes, until hot and bubbly. Let stand 5 minutes before serving.

Makes 2 casseroles, 4 servings each. Per serving: 541 calories, 21 grams protein, 84 grams carbohydrate, 12 grams fat, 25 milligrams cholesterol, 1,097 milligrams sodium

Microwave Method: Use microwave-safe baking dishes and do not line with foil. Assemble as above. Microwave one at a time. Cover with a lid or vented plastic wrap and microwave on high 10 to 15 minutes, rotating dish ½ turn once. Let stand 3 to 5 minutes to equalize temperature before serving.

Pumpkin-Stuffed Shells

An unusual and delectable version of Italian-style stuffed shells.

36 jumbo-size pasta shells (about 9 ounces)
1 jar (about 32 ounces) spaghetti sauce
1 large egg
1 can (16 ounces) solid-pack pumpkin
½ cup packaged Italian-style dry bread crumbs
½ cup grated Parmesan cheese
¼ teaspoon ground nutmeg
2 cups shredded mozzarella cheese (8 ounces)

1. Bring a large pot of water to a boil over high heat. Add pasta shells and cook according to package directions, stirring frequently but gently, until firm to the bite. Drain in a colander and rinse gently under cold running water. Drain upside down in a single layer on paper towels.

2. Heat oven to 350°F. Have a 13x9x2-inch baking dish ready.

3. Spoon a thin layer of sauce into bottom of baking dish.

4. Lightly beat egg in a medium-size bowl. Stir in pumpkin, bread crumbs, Parmesan cheese and nutmeg until blended.

5. Stuff pasta shells with pumpkin mixture and arrange stuffed side down in a single layer over sauce. Pour remaining sauce over shells. Cover tightly with foil and bake 30 minutes.

6. Remove foil. Sprinkle mozzarella cheese evenly over top and bake uncovered 10 to 15 minutes longer, until cheese melts and sauce is bubbling. Serve immediately.

Makes 6 servings. Per serving: 494 calories, 22 grams protein, 65 grams carbohydrate, 16 grams fat, 70 milligrams cholesterol, 1,303 milligrams sodium

Stuffed Manicotti

Stuffed Manicotti

Manicotti are large tubular pasta. This recipe makes two pans of manicotti, enough for two meals. If you like, line one of the pans with heavy-duty foil and freeze unbaked for another meal (see Note).

Sauce
  2 tablespoons olive oil
  1½ teaspoons minced fresh garlic
  2 cans (35 ounces each) Italian plum tomatoes, drained and broken up
  2 teaspoons dried basil leaves
  ½ teaspoon dried marjoram leaves
  ¼ teaspoon salt
  ⅛ teaspoon pepper

Pasta and Filling
  16 manicotti (about 9 ounces)
  1½ pounds Italian sausage, removed from casings
  2 containers (15 ounces each) ricotta cheese
  2 tablespoons grated Parmesan cheese
  1 large egg
  2 cups shredded mozzarella cheese (8 ounces)

1. To make sauce: Heat oil in a large skillet over medium-high heat. Add garlic and cook 1 to 2 minutes, stirring frequently, until lightly golden. Stir in tomatoes, herbs, salt and pepper and bring to a simmer. Reduce heat to medium and simmer uncovered 20 minutes, stirring frequently, until sauce is slightly thickened. Remove from heat.

2. Meanwhile, bring a large pot of water to a boil over high heat. Add manicotti and cook according to package directions, gently stirring a few times, until firm to the bite. Drain in a colander and rinse gently under cold running water, being careful not to tear manicotti. (If they start to stick, toss with a little olive oil.)

3. Crumble sausage into a large skillet. Brown over medium heat, breaking up meat with a wooden spoon. Drain off fat and put sausage in a medium-size bowl. Let cool 5 minutes.

4. Add ricotta, Parmesan and egg to sausage and stir until blended.

5. Heat oven to 375°F. Have two shallow 2-quart baking dishes ready. Spread ¼ cup of the sauce in each dish.

6. Fill each manicotti with about 2 tablespoons sausage mixture. Arrange 8 stuffed manicotti in a single layer over sauce in each baking dish. Top each dish with half the remaining sauce (about 2 cups).

7. Cover baking dishes with foil. Bake 30 minutes, until hot and bubbly. Uncover and sprinkle top of each with 1 cup of the mozzarella. Bake 15 minutes longer, until cheese is melted and lightly browned.

Makes 8 servings. Per serving: 640 calories, 30 grams protein, 33 grams carbohydrate, 40 grams fat, 137 milligrams cholesterol, 793 milligrams sodium

Note: To freeze, line one baking dish with enough heavy-duty foil to bring up over and cover contents. Cover with foil and freeze unbaked in baking dish. When manicotti are frozen, remove from dish and wrap tightly. Return to freezer. Freeze remaining 1 cup shredded mozzarella cheese separately in plastic bag or container. To bake, heat oven to 375°F. Unwrap frozen manicotti and put back in baking dish. (No need to thaw.) Cover dish with foil and bake 45 minutes, until hot and bubbly. Meanwhile, remove mozzarella from freezer. Uncover manicotti and sprinkle with mozzarella. Bake 15 minutes longer, until cheese is melted and lightly browned.

Macaroni and Cheese

To keep the calories under control, we used reduced-calorie cheese—and less of it—and broth and evaporated skimmed milk instead of whole milk or cream.

    6 ounces elbow macaroni (about
        1½ cups)
    ¼ cup minced onion
    6 ounces (9 slices, ⅔ ounce each)
        reduced-calorie sharp Cheddar-
        flavor processed cheese
    1 can (12 ounces) evaporated
        skimmed milk
    ½ cup chicken broth
    2½ tablespoons all-purpose flour
    ½ teaspoon dry mustard
    ¼ teaspoon Worcestershire sauce
    ⅛ teaspoon pepper
    3 tablespoons packaged dry
        bread crumbs
    1 tablespoon margarine, at room
        temperature

1. Heat oven to 375°F. Spray a deep 2-quart casserole with vegetable cooking spray.

2. Bring a medium-size pot of water to a boil over high heat. Add macaroni and cook according to package directions, stirring frequently, until firm to the bite. Drain in a colander.

3. Layer one third of the macaroni in prepared casserole, then half the onion and cheese. Repeat layers, ending with macaroni.

4. Whisk milk, broth, flour, dry mustard, Worcestershire sauce and pepper in a medium-size bowl until well blended. Pour into casserole. Mix bread crumbs and margarine with a fork or your fingers and sprinkle over casserole. Bake 30 minutes, until hot and bubbly. Serve.

Makes 4 servings. Per serving: 374 calories, 25 grams protein, 53 grams carbohydrate, 7 grams fat, 23 milligrams cholesterol, 942 milligrams sodium

Savory Noodle Pudding

A lovely accompaniment to roast chicken or baked ham.

    8 ounces medium-wide egg noodles
    1 cup chopped green onions
    2 tablespoons butter or margarine
    1½ cups cottage cheese
    3 large eggs, lightly beaten
    1 tablespoon poppy seed
    1 teaspoon salt
    ⅛ teaspoon pepper

1. Heat oven to 400°F. Grease a deep 2-quart casserole.

2. Bring a large pot of water to a boil over high heat. Add egg noodles and cook according to package directions, stirring frequently, until firm to the bite. Drain in a colander. Transfer to a large bowl.

3. Cook green onions in butter in a medium-size skillet over medium heat 2 minutes, until barely wilted. Add to noodles.

4. Add cottage cheese, eggs, poppy seed, salt and pepper to noodles and stir until well blended. Pour into prepared casserole.

5. Bake 30 minutes, until top is flecked with brown. Let stand 5 to 10 minutes before serving.

Makes 4 servings. Per serving: 437 calories, 23 grams protein, 46 grams carbohydrate, 17 grams fat, 248 milligrams cholesterol with butter, 230 milligrams cholesterol with margarine, 835 milligrams sodium

Macaroni and Cheese

Spaghetti Quiche

This quiche without a crust makes a wonderful and unusual brunch dish. Serve with pumpernickel-raisin bread and glasses of spicy tomato juice with celery-stalk stirrers.

8 ounces spaghetti
4 ounces sliced fully cooked ham, cut in 1-inch squares (about 1 cup)
1 cup diced red or green bell pepper
1 cup diced zucchini
2 cups milk
4 large eggs
½ cup grated Parmesan cheese
1 teaspoon salt
⅛ teaspoon pepper

1. Heat oven to 325°F. Grease a 12-inch quiche dish (not one with a removable bottom) or a shallow casserole.

2. Bring a large pot of water to a boil over high heat. Add spaghetti and cook 5 minutes, stirring frequently. Drain in a colander. (Spaghetti will cook further in dish.)

3. Transfer spaghetti to a medium-size bowl. Toss with ham, bell pepper and zucchini. Turn into prepared quiche dish. (Dish may be covered and refrigerated up to two days at this point.)

4. Beat milk, eggs, cheese, salt and pepper in a medium-size bowl. Pour over spaghetti mixture. Bake 50 minutes, until lightly browned and edges are set. Center will be soft. Let stand 10 minutes, until eggs are set and cooked. Cut in wedges and serve.

Makes 8 servings. Per serving: 245 calories, 14 grams protein, 26 grams carbohydrate, 9 grams fat, 123 milligrams cholesterol, 510 milligrams sodium

Herbed Pasta-Tuna Bake

Mayonnaise makes a creamy substitute for white sauce or condensed creamed soup in this hearty casserole.

8 ounces (about 2 cups) pasta shells
2 cans (6½ ounces each) tuna, drained and broken in chunks
½ cup chopped celery
3 cups loosely packed parsley sprigs (1 large bunch)
⅔ cup coarsely chopped green onions
½ cup mayonnaise
½ cup milk

1. Heat oven to 400°F. Grease a deep 2-quart casserole.

2. Bring a large pot of water to a boil over high heat. Add pasta shells and cook according to package directions, stirring frequently, until firm to the bite. Drain in a colander.

3. Mix shells, tuna and celery in prepared casserole.

4. Process parsley, green onions, mayonnaise and milk in a food processor or blender until smooth. Pour over tuna mixture and toss to coat. Bake 15 minutes, until bubbly. Stir before serving.

Makes 4 servings. Per serving: 597 calories, 32 grams protein, 47 grams carbohydrate, 31 grams fat, 74 milligrams cholesterol, 820 milligrams sodium

Herbed Pasta-Tuna Bake

Ravioli and Tortellini

♥ LOW-CALORIE

Cheese Ravioli with Romaine-Tomato Sauce

A different and delicious use for a salad green.

1 package (about 15 ounces) frozen or
    fresh cheese ravioli
3 tablespoons vegetable oil
1 teaspoon minced fresh garlic
1 medium-size head (1 pound)
    romaine lettuce, rinsed, drained
    and cut in 1-inch crosswise slices
    (about 8 loosely packed cups)
1 can (14½ ounces) tomatoes, drained
    and broken up
½ teaspoon salt
¼ teaspoon pepper
2 tablespoons grated Parmesan cheese
⅓ cup toasted pumpkin seeds
    (optional; see Note)

1. Bring a large pot of water to a boil over high heat. Add ravioli and cook according to package directions, stirring frequently, until tender yet firm to the bite. Drain in a colander.

2. Meanwhile, heat oil in a large heavy saucepan over medium heat. Add garlic and cook about 1 minute, until golden. Add romaine. Cover and cook 5 minutes, stirring once or twice, until lettuce wilts.

3. Add tomatoes, salt and pepper. Raise heat to high. Cook uncovered 5 minutes, until some of the liquid evaporates.

4. Transfer ravioli to a large heated serving bowl. Pour sauce over ravioli and sprinkle with cheese and pumpkin seeds, if desired, and serve.

Makes 4 servings. Per serving (without pumpkin seeds): 248 calories, 9 grams protein, 24 grams carbohydrate, 14 grams fat, 65 milligrams cholesterol, 714 milligrams sodium

Note: Pumpkin seeds are available at most supermarkets and health-food stores. Toast in a small nonstick skillet over medium-high heat, shaking frequently, until light golden brown.

Cheese Ravioli with Vegetables

The frozen ravioli cooks right in the skillet with the sauce.

1 cup water
1 cup heavy cream
1 tablespoon vegetable oil
½ teaspoon dried basil leaves
⅛ teaspoon minced fresh garlic
1 package (about 15 ounces) frozen
    cheese ravioli (40 in a package),
    not thawed
1 can (10¾ ounces) condensed cream
    of spinach soup, undiluted
1 bag (16 ounces) frozen mixed
    broccoli, cauliflower and carrots,
    thawed and drained
⅛ teaspoon salt
⅛ teaspoon pepper

1. Bring water and cream to a boil in a large skillet, preferably nonstick, over high heat.

2. Stir in oil, basil and garlic. Stir in ravioli. Cover and return to a boil. Uncover, stir and reduce heat to low. Cover and simmer 7 minutes, then stir again.

3. Add soup, vegetables, salt and pepper to skillet and stir to blend. Raise heat to high and bring to a boil. Reduce heat to low and simmer uncovered 4 minutes, stirring twice to keep ravioli from sticking to skillet, until pasta is tender. Spoon into soup plates or a large heated serving bowl and serve.

Makes 4 servings. Per serving: 550 calories, 16 grams protein, 49 grams carbohydrate, 34 grams fat, 175 milligrams cholesterol, 648 milligrams sodium

Ravioli

Ravioli are squares or pillows of pasta dough filled with meat, cheese or vegetables to form little cushions. They are sold fresh or frozen.

Cheese Ravioli with Vegetables

Ravioli Primavera Casserole

⏱ MAKE-AHEAD

Ravioli Primavera Casserole

Children love this colorful dish.

- 1 package (about 17 ounces) fresh or frozen cheese ravioli
- 3 tablespoons butter or margarine
- 3 tablespoons all-purpose flour
- 2½ cups milk
- 2 cups frozen cut broccoli, partially thawed
- 1 small red bell pepper (4 ounces), cut in short thin strips (about 1 cup)
- 2 green onions, thinly sliced
- 1 teaspoon dried basil leaves
- ½ teaspoon dried oregano leaves
- ¼ teaspoon salt
- ¼ teaspoon pepper

1. Heat oven to 350°F. Grease a 2-quart baking dish.

2. Bring a large pot of water to a boil over high heat. Add ravioli and cook according to package directions, stirring frequently, until tender yet firm to the bite. Drain in a colander.

3. Meanwhile, melt butter in a medium-size saucepan over medium heat. Add flour and cook 2 to 3 minutes, stirring constantly, until bubbly. Gradually whisk in milk until smooth. Reduce heat to low and simmer 5 minutes, stirring occasionally, until sauce is thick.

4. Stir in broccoli, bell pepper, green onions, herbs, salt and pepper. Raise heat to medium and cook 5 minutes, until vegetables are crisp-tender. Remove from heat.

5. Add drained ravioli and toss to mix well. Spoon into prepared baking dish. (Dish may be cooled, covered and refrigerated up to two days at this point. Bake as directed.)

6. Cover and bake about 35 minutes, until hot and bubbly. Serve immediately.

Makes 4 servings. Per serving: 477 calories, 23 grams protein, 58 grams carbohydrate, 18 grams fat, 143 milligrams cholesterol with butter, 116 milligrams cholesterol with margarine, 575 milligrams sodium

One-Pot Tortellini with Vegetables

Look for fresh tortellini in your grocer's refrigerated section. You can use cheese tortellini instead of meat-filled tortellini.

- 1 bag (16 ounces) frozen mixed carrots, peas, zucchini, pearl onions, red peppers
- 2 packages (9 ounces each) fresh meat-filled tortellini
- ¼ cup olive oil
- 1 teaspoon minced fresh garlic
- ¼ teaspoon crushed red-pepper flakes
- ¼ cup grated Parmesan cheese
- 2 tablespoons chopped fresh parsley (optional)

1. Bring a large pot of water to a boil over high heat.

2. Rinse vegetables in a colander under warm running water until partially thawed and pieces can be separated. Stir vegetables and tortellini into boiling water. Cover and return to a boil. Uncover and boil 3 minutes, until tortellini are tender yet firm to the bite and vegetables are crisp-tender. Drain tortellini and vegetables in a colander.

3. Meanwhile, heat oil, garlic and crushed red pepper in a small saucepan over medium-low heat just until garlic starts to sizzle. Remove from heat.

4. Transfer tortellini and vegetables to a large heated serving bowl. Pour in hot garlic oil and sprinkle with Parmesan and parsley, if desired. Toss to coat and serve immediately.

Makes 4 servings. Per serving: 568 calories, 26 grams protein, 70 grams carbohydrate, 21 grams fat, 79 milligrams cholesterol, 717 milligrams sodium

One-Pot Tortellini with Vegetables

Tortellini with Spicy Meat Sauce

On the side: spinach salad tossed with Italian dressing.

- 12 ounces fresh or frozen cheese tortellini (4 generous cups)
- 8 ounces lean ground beef
- 1 cup marinara sauce (from a jar)
- 1 can (4 ounces) chopped green chiles, drained
- 1 teaspoon dried oregano leaves
- ¼ teaspoon crushed red-pepper flakes, or to taste

For garnish: chopped fresh parsley

1. Bring a large pot of water to a boil over high heat. Add tortellini and cook according to package directions, stirring frequently, until tender yet firm to the bite. Drain in a colander.

2. Meanwhile, crumble beef into a large skillet. Stir over high heat 3 minutes, until no longer pink. Pour off any fat.

3. Add marinara sauce, chiles, oregano and crushed red pepper to beef and stir until blended. Bring to a boil. Reduce heat to medium-low and simmer 4 minutes, stirring occasionally, until flavors are blended.

4. Transfer tortellini to a large heated serving bowl. Pour in sauce and toss. Sprinkle with parsley and serve.

Makes 4 servings. Per serving: 427 calories, 25 grams protein, 49 grams carbohydrate, 14 grams fat, 72 milligrams cholesterol, 784 milligrams sodium

---

Tortellini

Sold refrigerated in the dairy case or frozen, tortellini are a filled pasta that has been twisted to form a ring. They are stuffed with meat, vegetables or, most commonly, cheese.

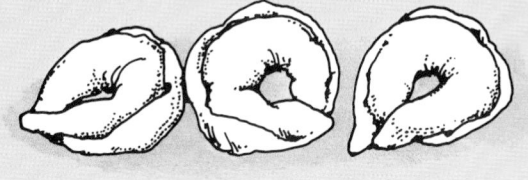

Double-Cheese Tortellini

Double-Cheese Tortellini

Serve with a crisp green salad dressed with a tangy vinaigrette.

- **12 ounces fresh or frozen cheese tortellini (4 generous cups)**
- **1 package (1-cup yield) white-sauce mix**
- **¾ cup milk**
- **8 ounces hot or mild processed cheese spread with jalapeño peppers, cut in small chunks**
- **8 ounces fully cooked ham, cut in small cubes (about 1⅓ cups)**
- **½ cup halved pitted ripe olives**
- **¾ teaspoon Worcestershire sauce**
- **2 tablespoons sliced green onions**

1. Bring a large pot of water to a boil over high heat. Add tortellini and cook according to package directions, stirring frequently, until tender yet firm to the bite. Drain in a colander.

2. Meanwhile, whisk sauce mix and milk in a medium-size saucepan over medium-high heat until mixture boils. Reduce heat to medium-low. Stir in cheese, ham, olives and Worcestershire sauce. Stir until cheese melts.

3. Transfer tortellini to a large heated serving bowl. Pour in sauce and toss to mix. Sprinkle with green onions and serve.

Makes 4 servings. Per serving: 706 calories, 46 grams protein, 60 grams carbohydrate, 34 grams fat, 158 milligrams cholesterol, 1,731 milligrams sodium

Tortellini with Mushrooms and Peas

Try this with tortellini made with egg or spinach pasta, or a colorful combination of the two.

- 1 teaspoon salt
- 2 packages (9 ounces each) fresh cheese tortellini (about 5 cups) or 1 bag (16 ounces) frozen
- 1 box (10 ounces) frozen green peas
- ¼ cup butter or margarine
- 8 ounces mushrooms, cut in quarters (about 2½ cups)
- 4 teaspoons cornstarch
- 1½ cups milk
- 2 tablespoons grated Parmesan cheese
- ¼ cup sliced green-onion tops

1. Bring a large pot of water to a boil over high heat. Add salt, then tortellini and cook 1 minute less than directed on package, stirring fre-quently. Add peas and return to a boil. Cook 1 minute, until peas are hot and tortellini are tender yet firm to the bite. Drain in a colander and rinse with warm water.

2. Meanwhile, melt butter in a large skillet over medium-high heat. Add mushrooms; cover and cook about 2 minutes, stirring once, until lightly browned.

3. Mix cornstarch and a few tablespoons of the milk in a small cup. Add remaining milk to skillet, then stir in cornstarch mixture. Raise heat to high and bring to a boil, stirring con-stantly, until sauce thickens. Remove from heat and stir in cheese and green-onion tops.

4. Transfer tortellini to a large heated serving bowl. Pour sauce over tortellini. Toss well and serve.

Makes 4 servings. Per serving: 590 calories, 29 grams protein, 72 grams carbohydrate, 21 grams fat, 96 milligrams cholesterol with butter, 60 milligrams cho-lesterol with margarine, 884 milligrams sodium

Tortellini with Mushrooms and Peas

Tortellini with Chile-Tomato Sauce

Garden-Style Tortellini

Tortellini with Chile-Tomato Sauce

A spicy Southwestern-inspired pasta dish.

- 1 teaspoon salt
- 2 packages (9 ounces each) fresh tortellini with meat (about 5 cups) or 1 bag (16 ounces) frozen tortellini
- 2 tablespoons pignoli (pine nuts, see Pignoli, page 21)
- 1 tablespoon olive oil
- ½ cup frozen or fresh chopped onion
- 1 to 2 tablespoons (to your taste) chopped, seeded, fresh or canned jalapeño peppers
- 1 teaspoon minced fresh garlic
- 1 can (about 16 ounces) tomatoes
- ½ cup heavy cream
- ½ cup sliced pitted ripe olives

1. Bring a large pot of water to a boil over high heat. Add salt, then tortellini and cook according to package directions, stirring frequently, until tender yet firm to the bite. Drain in a colander and rinse with warm water.

2. Meanwhile, put pignoli in a medium-size saucepan and toast over medium heat, shaking frequently, until lightly browned. Transfer to a small bowl.

3. Heat oil in same saucepan over medium-high heat. Add onion, jalapeño peppers and garlic. Cook about 2 minutes, stirring often, until onion is limp. Stir in tomatoes and their liquid, breaking up tomatoes with the back of a spoon. Bring to a boil. Reduce heat to medium-low and simmer about 5 minutes, until sauce is slightly thickened.

4. While sauce simmers, boil cream in a small saucepan over medium heat 3 minutes, until reduced by half. Stir cream into tomato sauce.

5. Transfer tortellini to a large heated serving bowl. Spoon sauce over tortellini. Sprinkle with pignoli and olives and serve immediately.

Makes 4 servings. Per serving: 607 calories, 26 grams protein, 69 grams carbohydrate, 26 grams fat, 128 milligrams cholesterol, 896 milligrams sodium

Garden-Style Tortellini

Vary this with other frozen-vegetable combinations. The recipe uses only one pot, so it saves time as well as elbow grease.

- 6 cups water
- 3 chicken bouillon cubes or 1 tablespoon instant chicken-broth granules
- 12 ounces fresh or frozen cheese tortellini (4 generous cups)
- 1 bag (16 ounces) frozen mixed broccoli, cauliflower and carrots
- ¼ cup olive oil
- 1 teaspoon minced fresh garlic
- ¼ cup grated Parmesan cheese

Pepper to taste

1. Put water, bouillon and tortellini in a large pot. Cover and bring to a boil over high heat.

2. Add vegetables, return liquid to a boil and cook uncovered 1 to 2 minutes, until vegetables are hot but still crisp and tortellini are tender yet firm to the bite. Drain vegetables and pasta in a colander, reserving ¼ cup cooking liquid.

3. Heat oil and garlic in the pasta cooking pot over medium heat, stirring constantly (don't let garlic brown). Add tortellini, vegetables and reserved liquid and toss to mix well.

4. Spoon tortellini into soup plates or bowls. Sprinkle each serving with cheese and pepper and serve.

Makes 4 servings. Per serving: 438 calories, 19 grams protein, 46 grams carbohydrate, 19 grams fat, 42 milligrams cholesterol, 1,168 milligrams sodium

Tortellini Primavera

The cheese and the broccoli make this dish a good source of calcium.

12 ounces fresh or frozen cheese
    tortellini (4 generous cups)
½ cup olive oil
¼ cup chopped onion
1 teaspoon minced fresh garlic
1 teaspoon crumbled dried
    thyme leaves
½ teaspoon salt, or to taste
¼ teaspoon pepper
1 package (16 ounces) frozen mixed
    broccoli, baby carrots and water
    chestnuts, partially thawed
1 large red bell pepper, cut in
    thin strips
8 cherry tomatoes, halved

1. Bring a large pot of water to a boil over high heat. Add tortellini and cook according to package directions, stirring frequently, until tender yet firm to the bite. Drain in a colander.

2. Meanwhile, heat oil in a large skillet over medium heat. Stir in onion, garlic, thyme, salt and pepper. Cook 2 minutes, until onion is nearly tender.

3. Add frozen mixed vegetables, bell pepper and cherry tomatoes and cook about 3 minutes, until vegetables are heated through.

4. Transfer tortellini to a large heated serving bowl. Pour vegetables over tortellini; toss to mix and serve.

Makes 4 servings. Per serving: 558 calories, 18 grams protein, 53 grams carbohydrate, 28 grams fat, 34 milligrams cholesterol, 680 milligrams sodium

Tortellini with Roasted Peppers and Snow-peas

12 ounces fresh or frozen cheese
    tortellini (4 generous cups)
4 ounces snow-peas, trimmed
⅓ cup olive or vegetable oil
2 tablespoons red-wine vinegar
2 teaspoons Dijon mustard
½ teaspoon salt
¼ teaspoon minced fresh garlic
¼ teaspoon dried marjoram or
    oregano leaves
Pepper to taste
⅓ cup diced roasted red peppers
    (from a jar)
¼ cup sliced green onions
Lettuce leaves

1. Bring a large pot of water to a boil over high heat. Add tortellini and cook according to package directions, stirring frequently, until tender yet firm to the bite. About 1 minute before pasta is done, add snow-peas and cook until crisp-tender. Drain tortellini and snow-peas in a colander.

2. Meanwhile whisk oil, vinegar, mustard, salt, garlic, marjoram and pepper in a large bowl until blended. Add hot tortellini and snow-peas, roasted peppers and green onions and toss.

3. Line plates with lettuce leaves. Spoon tortellini mixture over lettuce and serve.

Makes 4 servings. Per serving: 433 calories, 15 grams protein, 43 grams carbohydrate, 22 grams fat, 34 milligrams cholesterol, 681 milligrams sodium

Russian Pasta

Make this dish with pelmeni, a Russian pasta found in specialty shops, or substitute tortellini. Garnish with fresh dill instead of parsley for a touch of authenticity.

1 pound fresh or frozen pelmeni
    or tortellini
5 tablespoons butter or margarine
1 pound fresh ripe tomatoes, coarsely
    chopped, or 1 can (28 ounces)
    tomatoes, drained and chopped
¼ cup chopped dried tomatoes
    (optional; see Dried Tomatoes,
    page 9)
½ teaspoon salt
Pepper to taste
¼ cup sour cream
For garnish: chopped fresh parsley

1. Bring a large pot of water to a boil over high heat. Add pelmeni and cook according to package directions, stirring frequently, until tender yet firm to the bite. Drain in a colander.

2. Meanwhile, melt butter in a large skillet over medium heat. Add fresh and dried tomatoes, if desired, and cook 4 to 5 minutes, stirring occasionally, until sauce is thickened. Stir in salt and pepper.

3. Transfer pelmeni to a large heated serving bowl or soup plates. Spoon sauce over pasta. Top with sour cream and sprinkle with parsley. Serve.

Makes 4 servings. Per serving (with tortellini): 516 calories, 21 grams protein, 58 grams carbohydrate, 22 grams fat, 95 milligrams cholesterol with butter, 50 milligrams cholesterol with margarine, 951 milligrams sodium

Pasta
Salads

*Everybody needs lots of quick, easy
pasta-salad recipes for the picnic table, a party buffet
or a light summer supper.*

Mediterranean Pasta Salad

Vegetables

Mediterranean Pasta Salad

For a change of pace, substitute tuna for the cheese. This is a main-course salad, perfect for a summer supper.

12 ounces rotelle
⅔ cup olive oil
3 tablespoons red-wine vinegar
¼ cup chopped fresh basil leaves
2 tablespoons chopped green onion
2 tablespoons grated Parmesan
    cheese
1¼ teaspoons salt
¼ teaspoon pepper
1 *each* small red, green and yellow
    bell pepper, halved lengthwise
    and cut in thin crosswise strips
1 medium-size fresh tomato, cut in
    thin wedges
¼ cup toasted pignoli (pine nuts, see
    Pignoli, page 21)
¼ cup calamata or pitted ripe olives
8 ounces feta or mozzarella cheese,
    cubed
¼ teaspoon crumbled dried
    oregano leaves

1. Bring a large pot of water to a boil over high heat. Add rotelle and cook according to package directions, stirring frequently, until firm to the bite. Drain in a colander.

2. Put oil, vinegar, 2 tablespoons of the basil, the green onion, Parmesan, salt and pepper in a blender or food processor and process until smooth.

3. Put pasta, bell-pepper strips, tomato wedges, pignoli and olives in a large bowl. Pour in dressing and toss to mix.

4. Roll cheese cubes in remaining 2 tablespoons basil to coat. Add to salad and sprinkle with oregano. Toss lightly. Let cool to room temperature or chill until ready to serve.

Makes 4 servings. Per serving (with feta cheese): 863 calories, 21 grams protein, 72 grams carbohydrate, 55 grams fat, 53 milligrams cholesterol, 1,442 milligrams sodium

Greek Pasta Salad

This salad is best eaten the day it is made. The pasta is cooked in the same water as the broccoli. For dessert: juicy slices of watermelon.

Salt
8 ounces fresh broccoli, trimmed, cut
    in small florets, stems peeled and
    cut in thin rounds (about 2½ cups)
8 ounces rotini
4 ounces mushrooms, quartered
    (about 2 cups)
1 cup crumbled feta cheese (4 ounces)
4 ounces oil-cured black olives (1 cup)
⅓ cup pignoli (pine nuts) or walnuts,
    toasted (see Pignoli, page 21)
¼ teaspoon pepper
1 cup olive oil
¼ cup freshly squeezed lemon juice
1 can (2 ounces) flat anchovy fillets,
    drained

1. Bring a large pot of water to a boil over high heat. Add salt to taste, then add broccoli. Cook 2 to 3 minutes, stirring occasionally, until crisp-tender. Remove broccoli with a strainer; cool under cold running water. Drain well.

2. Return water to a boil. Add rotini and cook according to package directions, stirring frequently, until firm to the bite. Drain in a colander. Rinse under cold running water and shake to remove excess water.

3. Put pasta, broccoli, mushrooms, feta, olives, pignoli and pepper in a large bowl. Toss to mix.

4. To make dressing: Put olive oil, lemon juice and anchovies in a food processor or a blender and process until smooth. Pour dressing over salad; toss to coat and serve or cover and refrigerate up to 2 hours.

Makes 8 servings. Per serving: 479 calories, 10 grams protein, 27 grams carbohydrate, 38 grams fat, 16 milligrams cholesterol, 677 milligrams sodium

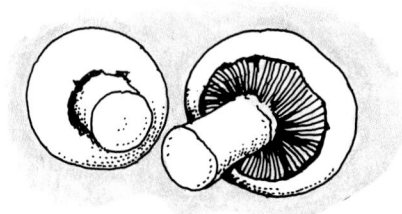

Pasta, Snow-pea and Tomato Salad

A lovely fresh pasta salad that is good with grilled chicken or hamburgers.

- **8 ounces snow-peas or sugar-snap peas, trimmed**
- **12 ounces medium-size pasta shells**
- **¼ cup red-wine vinegar**
- **1 teaspoon salt**
- **Pepper to taste**
- **½ cup vegetable oil**
- **1 pint basket cherry tomatoes, halved**

1. Bring a large pot of water to a boil. Add peas and cook 1 to 2 minutes, until crisp-tender and bright green. Remove with a strainer and cool peas under cold running water. Drain well.

2. Return water to a boil and add pasta shells. Cook according to package directions, stirring frequently, until pasta is firm to the bite. Drain in a colander and cool under cold running water. Shake off excess water.

3. Meanwhile, whisk vinegar, salt and pepper in a large serving bowl. Slowly beat in oil until blended. Add pasta and tomatoes and toss gently to coat. Marinate at least 15 minutes, tossing occasionally. Refrigerate or serve within 1 hour. Just before serving, add peas and toss to mix.

Makes 6 servings, about 1⅔ cups each. Per serving: 401 calories, 9 grams protein, 49 grams carbohydrate, 19 grams fat, 0 milligrams cholesterol, 184 milligrams sodium

Noodle-and-Pepper Salad with Basil Dressing

Charles Pinsky, who produces many of the popular cooking shows for Public Television, contributed this recipe to *Woman's Day*. If fresh basil is not available, substitute 1 cup Italian parsley sprigs and 1 teaspoon dried basil leaves.

- **8 ounces fettuccine**
- **1 cup packed fresh basil leaves**
- **2 tablespoons red-wine vinegar**
- **2 tablespoons water**
- **1 teaspoon salt**
- **1 teaspoon minced fresh garlic**
- **Pepper to taste**
- **½ cup olive oil**
- **2 large green or yellow bell peppers, or a combination, cut in chunks**
- **For garnish: fresh basil leaves**

1. Bring a large pot of water to a boil. Add fettuccine and cook according to package directions, stirring frequently, until firm to the bite. Drain in a colander and cool under cold running water. Shake off excess water.

2. Put basil, vinegar, water, salt, garlic and pepper in a food processor or blender. Process until basil is finely chopped. With machine running, slowly pour in oil and process until creamy.

3. Transfer fettuccine to a large serving bowl. Pour dressing over noodles and toss to coat. Cover and marinate at least 10 minutes, tossing occasionally. Refrigerate or serve within 1 hour. Just before serving, add bell peppers and toss to mix. Garnish with fresh basil leaves and serve.

Makes 6 servings, about 1 cup each. Per serving: 300 calories, 5 grams protein, 29 grams carbohydrate, 20 grams fat, 15 milligrams cholesterol, 183 milligrams sodium

Fusilli with Fresh Tomato Salad

Johanne Killeen, who owns the Al Forno restaurant in Providence, Rhode Island, created this recipe for *Woman's Day*. She serves this side dish with grilled lamb or beef. Its flavor depends on perfectly ripe summer tomatoes.

12 **ounces fusilli or rotelle**
 4 **medium-size–to–large ripe fresh tomatoes, coarsely chopped (about 2 cups)**
¾ **cup virgin olive oil**
½ **cup chopped mixed fresh herbs (Italian parsley, basil, oregano and marjoram; see Notes)**
¼ **cup sliced green onions**
¼ **balsamic or malt vinegar (see Notes)**
¾ **teaspoon salt**
¼ **teaspoon pepper**

1. Bring a large pot of water to a boil over high heat. Add fusilli and cook according to package directions, stirring frequently, until firm to the bite. Drain in a colander.

2. Mix tomatoes, oil, herbs, green onions, vinegar, salt and pepper in a large bowl. Add pasta and toss well to coat. Let cool to room temperature before serving.

Makes 6 side-dish servings. Per serving: 469 calories, 8 grams protein, 47 grams carbohydrate, 28 grams fat, 0 milligrams cholesterol, 271 milligrams sodium

Notes: If an assortment of fresh herbs is not available, use mostly fresh parsley and/or basil chopped with 1 tablespoon dried oregano or marjoram leaves.

Look for balsamic vinegar, an aged fine wine vinegar with an herb-flavored base, in supermarkets or specialty-food stores.

Fusilli with Fresh Tomato Salad

Pasta and Grapefruit Salad

A light but filling luncheon dish for two or dinner side dish for four.

- 2 cups wheel-shaped pasta, small shells or rotelle
- 1 envelope (0.6 ounces) zesty Italian salad-dressing mix, prepared according to package directions
- ½ cup cut green beans, cooked crisp-tender
- 2 tablespoons diced red bell pepper
- ½ teaspoon dried basil leaves
- ¼ teaspoon pepper
- 12 small whole mushrooms or 6 medium-size mushrooms, halved
- 1 medium-size grapefruit, peeled, white membrane removed and sectioned

For garnish: lettuce leaves

1. Bring a medium-size pot of water to a boil over high heat. Add pasta wheels and cook according to package directions, stirring frequently, until firm to the bite. Drain in a colander and rinse under cold running water. Shake off excess water. Transfer to a medium-size serving bowl.

2. Add ½ cup of the prepared dressing, the green beans, bell pepper, basil and pepper to pasta and toss to mix. Cover and refrigerate about 1 hour to develop flavor.

3. Just before serving, add mushrooms and grapefruit and toss lightly to mix. Arrange lettuce leaves on a serving platter and spoon salad on top. Pass remaining dressing in a small bowl or sauce boat to spoon over each serving.

Makes 4 servings. Per serving (without additional dressing): 305 calories, 5 grams protein, 32 grams carbohydrate, 19 grams fat, 0 milligrams cholesterol, 278 milligrams sodium

Pasta and Cheese Salad with Soy-Ginger Dressing

This is best served freshly made and warm. You can also make this salad with broccoli rabe, a pungent green vegetable that looks like long, thin stalks of broccoli, or with Swiss chard.

- 2 cups small broccoli florets
- 8 ounces whole-wheat elbow macaroni or ziti
- 3 tablespoons soy sauce
- 3 tablespoons cider vinegar
- ¾ teaspoon ground ginger, or to taste
- 1 large clove garlic, minced
- 2 dashes hot-pepper sauce
- ⅓ cup vegetable oil
- 2 tablespoons minced green onions
- 1 large red bell pepper, cut in thin strips
- 8 ounces part-skim mozzarella cheese, cut in 1½ x ¼-inch strips

1. Bring a large pot of water to a boil over high heat. Add broccoli and cook 2 to 3 minutes, until crisp-tender. Remove broccoli with a slotted spoon or a strainer and rinse briefly under cold running water, just enough to stop the cooking but not to cool broccoli completely. Drain well.

2. Return water to a boil. Add the macaroni and cook according to package directions, stirring frequently, until firm to the bite. Drain in a colander.

3. Whisk soy sauce, vinegar, ginger, garlic and hot-pepper sauce in a large salad bowl until well blended. Beat in oil and green onions.

4. Add warm pasta, broccoli, red-pepper strips and cheese and toss to mix. Serve warm or at room temperature.

Makes 4 servings. Per serving: 592 calories, 27 grams protein, 59 grams carbohydrate, 28 grams fat, 30 milligrams cholesterol, 1,308 milligrams sodium

Japanese Cold Thin Noodles

⏱ MAKE-AHEAD
Japanese Cold Thin Noodles

Food writer Elizabeth Andoh uses authentic Japanese ingredients for this dish: *somen* (thin white wheat noodles), *dashi* (basic soup stock) and *mikan* (canned sliced oranges). We substituted some more easily available ingredients. In Japan the noodles are served separately on ice in a crystal bowl; the sauce ingredients are in cups for dipping. The tinkling of ice against glass makes the dish even sound cool. This salad is delicious served with simple broiled fish or chicken.

1½ **cups chicken broth**
3½ **tablespoons soy sauce**
  2 **tablespoons granulated sugar**
1½ **tablespoons mirin (rice wine) or**
    dry sherry

  1 **tablespoon grated fresh gingerroot**
  8 **ounces soba (buckwheat noodles)**
    or whole-wheat spaghetti,
    cooked, drained and chilled
  1 **cup thinly sliced cucumber**
  1 **can (11 ounces) mandarin oranges,**
    drained
¼ **cup fresh coriander or mint leaves**

1. Mix broth, soy sauce, sugar and mirin in a small saucepan. Heat about 1 minute, stirring constantly, until sugar dissolves. Add gingerroot and refrigerate until chilled.

2. To serve, put noodles in a large serving bowl. Pour chilled sauce over noodles and add cucumber, oranges and coriander. Toss to coat well and serve.

Makes 4 side-dish servings. Per serving (with whole-wheat spaghetti): 250 calories, 10 grams protein, 53 grams carbohydrate, 1 gram fat, 5 milligrams cholesterol, 1,431 milligrams sodium

Vermicelli with Onions Oriental

This unusual side dish or first course will give your guests a pleasant surprise. Great with grilled or broiled lamb, beef or chicken.

---

8 ounces vermicelli
4 tablespoons olive oil
2 teaspoons curry powder, or to taste
1 teaspoon ground coriander
½ teaspoon ground cardamom or the seeds from 4 cardamom pods
2 teaspoons minced fresh garlic
1 teaspoon salt
1 cup beef or chicken broth
8 ounces thawed frozen pearl onions (about 30)
½ cup golden raisins
¼ cup chopped fresh parsley
¼ cup pignoli (pine nuts, see Pignoli, page 21)
½ teaspoon pepper

1. Bring a large pot of water to a boil over high heat. Add vermicelli and cook according to package directions, stirring frequently, until firm to the bite. Drain in a colander and rinse under cold running water. Shake off excess water and transfer to a large bowl. Toss with 1 tablespoon of the oil. Cover and refrigerate.

2. Heat remaining 3 tablespoons oil in a large skillet over medium heat. Stir in curry powder, coriander and cardamom and cook 2 minutes.

3. Stir garlic and salt, then broth and onions into skillet. Cook 5 minutes, stirring occasionally, until onions are crisp-tender. Remove onions to a medium-size bowl with a slotted spoon.

4. Add raisins to skillet and simmer 5 minutes. Pour over onions. Stir in parsley, pignoli and pepper. Cover and let stand at room temperature 3 to 4 hours for flavor to develop. Toss with vermicelli and serve.

Makes 6 side-dish servings. Per serving: 298 calories, 7 grams protein, 42 grams carbohydrate, 12 grams fat, 0 milligrams cholesterol, 365 milligrams sodium

Vermicelli with Onions Oriental

Poultry

Garlic Chicken Salad with Whole-Wheat Spaghetti

A spicy main-dish salad. Serve on a warm day with tall glasses of iced tea.

- 8 ounces whole-wheat spaghetti
- 4 tablespoons Oriental sesame oil
- Salt
- 12 ounces boned and skinned chicken-breast halves
- ¼ cup rice-wine vinegar or cider vinegar
- 3 tablespoons vegetable oil
- 2 tablespoons soy sauce
- 2 tablespoons chili oil (see Note)
- 2 tablespoons minced fresh garlic
- ¼ teaspoon crushed red-pepper flakes, or to taste
- 1 large red or green bell pepper, cut in thin strips (about 1 cup)
- ¼ cup chopped green-onion tops
- 2 tablespoons chopped fresh cilantro
- 2 cups shredded Chinese cabbage (napa) or spinach leaves (5 ounces)
- For garnish: 8 tomato wedges

1. Bring a large pot of water to a boil over high heat. Add spaghetti and cook according to package directions, stirring frequently, until firm to the bite. Drain in a colander and transfer to a large bowl. Toss with 1 tablespoon of the sesame oil to prevent sticking and let cool to room temperature.

2. Bring a medium-size pot of salted water to a boil over high heat. Add chicken. Reduce heat to low, cover and simmer 10 minutes, until chicken is no longer pink in the center. Drain, let cool and tear into long shreds.

3. Whisk remaining 3 tablespoons sesame oil, the vinegar, vegetable oil and soy sauce in a small bowl. Add chicken and marinate 10 minutes at room temperature.

4. Add chicken with marinade to spaghetti and toss to mix.

5. Heat chili oil in a small skillet over medium-high heat. Add garlic and crushed red pepper and cook 30 seconds, stirring constantly. Stir in bell pepper and green-onion tops and cook 1 minute longer. Pour over spaghetti, add cilantro and toss.

6. Line platter with cabbage and mound salad on top. Garnish with tomato wedges and serve.

Makes 4 servings. Per serving: 609 calories, 36 grams protein, 48 grams carbohydrate, 31 grams fat, 67 milligrams cholesterol, 731 milligrams sodium

Note: Chili oil is available in supermarket Oriental-specialty food sections.

Sesame Noodles with Chicken and Broccoli

If you wish, start the meal with a cup of hot soup and end with lemon sherbet sprinkled with coconut.

- 2 cups broccoli florets
- 8 ounces linguine
- 1 tablespoon vegetable oil
- ½ cup smooth peanut butter
- ¼ cup soy sauce
- 2 tablespoons red-wine vinegar
- 2 tablespoons Oriental sesame oil
- 2 teaspoons granulated sugar
- 2 cloves garlic, minced
- ½ teaspoon ground red pepper
- For garnish: sliced green onion
- 8 ounces cold cooked chicken, cut or torn in strips
- 2 cups cherry tomatoes, halved

1. Bring a large pot of water to a boil over high heat. Add broccoli and cook about 2 minutes, until crisp-tender. Remove from water with a strainer and cool under cold running water. Drain well.

2. Return water to a boil. Add linguine and cook according to package directions, stirring frequently, until firm to the bite. Drain in a colander, reserving ½ cup of cooking water, and rinse under cold running water. Toss with vegetable oil to prevent sticking.

3. Whisk peanut butter and the reserved pasta cooking water in a large bowl until smooth. Whisk in soy sauce, vinegar, sesame oil, sugar, garlic and ground red pepper. Add linguine and toss to coat well.

4. Mound linguine in the center of a serving platter. Sprinkle with green onion. Surround with chicken, broccoli and tomatoes and serve.

Makes 4 servings. Per serving: 645 calories, 38 grams protein, 61 grams carbohydrate, 30 grams fat, 45 milligrams cholesterol, 1,571 milligrams sodium

Chicken and Pasta Salad with Herbed Tomato Marinade

⏱ MAKE-AHEAD

Chicken and Pasta Salad with Herbed Tomato Marinade

2 **packages (9 ounces each)
fresh linguine**

2 **pounds firm-ripe fresh tomatoes,
peeled (see Peeling Tomatoes,
page 10), seeded and cut in
½-inch pieces (about 4 cups)**

½ **cup minced sweet white or
red onion**

3 **tablespoons finely chopped
fresh parsley**

⅔ **cup olive oil**

½ **cup tomato juice**

1½ **tablespoons coarsely chopped fresh
oregano leaves or 1½ teaspoons
dried oregano**

2 **large cloves garlic, cut in pieces**

1¼ **teaspoons whole black
peppercorns, coarsely crushed
(see Note)**

1 **pound cooked chicken, torn in
small shreds (about 3½ cups)**

1. Bring a large pot of water to a boil over high heat. Add linguine and cook according to package directions, stirring frequently, until firm to the bite. Drain in a colander.

2. Mix tomatoes, onion and parsley in a large bowl.

3. Put oil, tomato juice, oregano, garlic and peppercorns in a blender and process until smooth. Pour over tomato mixture and stir until blended.

4. Add linguine and chicken. Gently toss to mix and coat. Cover and let stand up to 1 hour at room temperature or refrigerate several hours or overnight. Toss again before serving.

Makes 8 servings, 16 cups. Per serving: 515 calories, 26 grams protein, 53 grams carbohydrate, 21 grams fat, 48 milligrams cholesterol, 78 milligrams sodium

Note: To crush peppercorns, put them in a heavy plastic bag and crush with the smooth side of a meat mallet, a rolling pin or the bottom of a heavy saucepan.

Vegetable-Chicken Pasta Salad

Leftover turkey, ham or even salami can be used instead of the chicken.

- **5 ounces tubettini or other small pasta (¾ cup)**
- **8 ounces green beans, trimmed and cut in 1-inch pieces (about 2 cups)**
- **⅓ cup mayonnaise or salad dressing**
- **⅓ cup plain low-fat yogurt**
- **2 tablespoons lemon juice**
- **2 teaspoons Dijon mustard or prepared white horseradish**
- **1 teaspoon salt**
- **¼ teaspoon pepper**
- **8 ounces cooked chicken, torn in shreds (about 1¾ cups)**
- **1 cup thinly sliced red radishes**
- **½ cup chopped fresh parsley**

1. Bring a large pot of water to a boil over high heat. Add tubettini and green beans. Cook 8 to 10 minutes, stirring occasionally, until pasta is firm to the bite and beans are crisp-tender. Drain in a colander. Rinse under cold running water and shake off excess water.

2. Whisk mayonnaise, yogurt, lemon juice, mustard, salt and pepper in a large bowl. Add pasta and green beans, chicken, radishes and parsley. Mix gently to coat. Serve immediately or refrigerate up to 24 hours.

Makes 4 servings. Per serving: 390 calories, 25 grams protein, 33 grams carbohydrate, 17 grams fat, 59 milligrams cholesterol, 733 milligrams sodium

Vegetable-Chicken Pasta Salad

Chicken and Pasta Salad with Pesto

Make the pesto and prepare salad ingredients up to a day ahead, but don't toss them together more than eight hours before serving. If cooking pasta ahead, toss with a little oil after draining to prevent sticking; cover and refrigerate.

> 4 ounces (2 cups) rotelle
> 2 cups loosely packed torn
>   basil leaves
> 1 cup loosely packed Italian parsley
>   sprigs, thick stems removed
> ½ cup olive or vegetable oil
> 2 tablespoons water
> 1 tablespoon coarsely chopped
>   fresh garlic
> ½ cup grated Parmesan cheese
> 2½ cups coarsely shredded
>   cooked chicken
> 1 large zucchini (10 ounces), halved
>   lengthwise and cut crosswise in
>   ¼-inch-thick slices (about
>   2½ cups)
> 2 medium-size yellow bell peppers,
>   cut in ¼-inch strips (about
>   2 cups)
> **For garnish: fresh basil sprig**

1. Bring a medium-size saucepan of water to a boil over high heat. Add rotelle and cook according to package directions, stirring frequently, until firm to the bite. Drain in a colander and rinse under cold running water. Shake to remove excess water. Transfer to a large serving bowl.

2. Put basil, parsley, oil, water and garlic in a food processor or a blender and process until puréed. Add cheese and process just to mix.

3. To serve: Add chicken, zucchini and peppers to pasta and toss to mix. Add half the pesto and toss to coat well. Garnish with basil sprig. Pour remaining pesto into sauce boat to spoon over each serving.

Makes 4 servings. Per serving: 617 calories, 46 grams protein, 29 grams carbohydrate, 35 grams fat, 101 milligrams cholesterol, 183 milligrams sodium

Chicken, Broccoli and Pasta with Basil Mayonnaise

Try green beans or zucchini instead of broccoli or use a mixture of all three. Toast the walnuts for the Basil Mayonnaise in the oven while the chicken cooks.

> 2 whole chicken breasts (about
>   1 pound each)
> 1 tablespoon butter or margarine,
>   melted
> 8 ounces rotelle or penne
> 3 cups small broccoli florets
> 1 cup mayonnaise
> ½ cup walnuts, toasted
> ½ cup packed fresh basil leaves
> ½ cup freshly grated Parmesan cheese
> 1 tablespoon lemon juice
> 2 teaspoons coarsely chopped fresh
>   garlic
> 2 medium-size fresh tomatoes, cut in
>   wedges

1. Heat oven to 375°F. Have a small roasting pan ready.

2. Arrange chicken breasts in a single layer in roasting pan. Brush with butter. Bake 20 to 25 minutes, until chicken is springy to the touch and no longer pink in the center.

3. Chill chicken until cool enough to handle. Tear meat in narrow strips, discarding skin and bones.

4. Meanwhile, bring a large pot of water to a boil over high heat. Add rotelle and cook according to package directions, stirring frequently, until almost tender. Add broccoli to pot with pasta. Cook 2 minutes, until broccoli is crisp-tender and rotelle is firm to the bite. Drain pasta and broccoli in a colander. Cool under cold running water. Shake to remove excess water.

5. To make the dressing: Put mayonnaise, walnuts, basil, Parmesan, lemon juice and garlic in a food processor or blender. Process until smooth.

6. Transfer pasta and broccoli to a large salad bowl. Add chicken strips and tomatoes and Basil Mayonnaise. Toss to coat well and serve.

Makes 6 servings. Per serving: 663 calories, 28 grams protein, 37 grams carbohydrate, 46 grams fat, 77 milligrams cholesterol with butter, 71 milligrams cholesterol with margarine, 345 milligrams sodium

Meta

⏱ MAKE-AHEAD

Pasta Salad with Salami and Vegetables

This main-dish salad is best eaten just after cooling to room temperature. If you refrigerate it, let stand at room temperature about an hour before serving and toss with a few tablespoons hot water to make the dressing creamy again.

- 8 ounces snow-peas, trimmed
- 12 ounces penne or rotelle
- ½ cup mayonnaise
- 2 tablespoons lemon juice
- 1 teaspoon salt
- ½ teaspoon pepper
- 8 ounces hard salami, sliced ¼ inch thick and cut in ¼-inch-wide strips
- 2 medium-size carrots, shredded (about 1½ cups)
- 1 medium-size red bell pepper, cut in thin strips (about 1 cup)

1. Bring a large pot of water to a boil over high heat. Add snow-peas and cook about 1 minute, just until crisp-tender and bright green. Remove with a strainer and cool under cold running water. Drain well.

2. Return water to a boil. Add penne and cook according to package directions, stirring frequently, until firm to the bite. Drain in a colander and rinse briefly under cold running water. Shake to remove excess water.

3. Mix mayonnaise, lemon juice, salt and pepper in a large bowl. Add salami, carrots, bell pepper and snow-peas and toss to coat. Add pasta and toss until well blended. Serve at room temperature.

Makes 8 servings. Per serving: 408 calories, 13 grams protein, 38 grams carbohydrate, 23 grams fat, 28 milligrams cholesterol, 713 milligrams sodium

Pasta Salad with Salami and Vegetables

Curried Ham and Pasta Salad

🕐 **MAKE-AHEAD**

Curried Ham and Pasta Salad

If you prefer, coarsely chop the eggs and add with the ham.

---

    6 ounces wide egg noodles
    1 cup mayonnaise
  ½ cup sour cream
    2 tablespoons milk
    1 tablespoon curry powder
1¼ teaspoons salt
Pepper to taste
    8 ounces fully cooked ham, cut in
        1x½-inch strips (about 1½ cups)
  ½ pint basket cherry tomatoes, halved
  ¼ cup thinly sliced green onions
    4 hard-cooked eggs, halved (see
        Perfect Hard-Cooked Eggs, this
        page)
    1 package (10 ounces) frozen
        asparagus spears, thawed

1. Bring a large pot of water to a boil over high heat. Add noodles and cook according to package directions, stirring frequently, until firm to the bite. Drain in a colander and rinse under cold running water. Shake off excess water.

2. Mix mayonnaise, sour cream, milk, curry powder, salt and pepper in a large bowl. Add noodles and toss with dressing. Add ham, tomatoes and green onions and stir to coat evenly.

3. Cover tightly and refrigerate 3 hours or overnight. Spoon salad onto serving plates or platter. Garnish plates with eggs and asparagus and serve.

Makes 4 servings. Per serving: 841 calories, 31 grams protein, 39 grams carbohydrate, 63 grams fat, 334 milligrams cholesterol, 1,593 milligrams sodium

---

Perfect Hard-Cooked Eggs

☐ Place eggs in a saucepan and add cold water to cover. Add a big pinch of salt to the water. (The salt will not flavor the eggs but will keep the whites inside the shells if eggs crack while cooking.) Bring water to a boil over high heat. Reduce heat to low and simmer 11 minutes. Remove saucepan to the sink and run cold water into saucepan until eggs are cool. Crack shells once and roll the eggs around on a counter to break shells into little pieces. Shell eggs and rinse to remove any remaining bits of shell. If not using at once, place in a bowl of cold water, cover and refrigerate.

☐ If you are watching your cholesterol and fat, discard yolks from several or all of the eggs and just use the whites. Egg whites contain plenty of the egg flavor and no fat or cholesterol.

Seafood

Main-Dish Ziti and Tuna Salad

You can substitute cooked chicken, turkey or other leftover cold meat for the tuna. Serve with bread sticks or a crisp loaf of hot garlic bread.

8 ounces (about 2½ cups) ziti or other large tubular pasta
1 jar (7 ounces) roasted red peppers, drained and cut in thin strips
1 small red onion, halved lengthwise and thinly sliced
½ cup diced celery
½ cup frozen green peas, thawed and drained
⅓ cup (about 20) small pimiento-stuffed green olives
⅓ cup bottled Italian salad dressing
1 can (13 ounces) solid white tuna, drained and broken in chunks
Lettuce leaves (optional)

1. Bring a large pot of water to a boil over high heat. Add ziti and cook according to package directions, stirring frequently, until firm to the bite. Drain in a colander and cool under cold running water. Shake off excess water and transfer ziti to a large serving bowl.

2. Add peppers, onion, celery, peas, olives and dressing to pasta and toss to mix well. Gently fold in tuna. Line a platter or plates with lettuce leaves, if desired; spoon salad over lettuce and serve.

Makes 6 servings. Per serving: 295 calories, 15 grams protein, 35 grams carbohydrate, 11 grams fat, 18 milligrams cholesterol, 547 milligrams sodium

Pasta-Tuna-Fruit Salad with Pimiento Dressing

This is a lovely light main course for lunch or supper on a hot day. The fresh fruit adds a cooling touch.

½ cup vegetable oil
¼ cup cider vinegar
2 teaspoons prepared mustard
½ teaspoon salt
1 large roasted red pepper (from a jar), drained and chopped
¼ cup sliced green onions
1 small clove garlic, minced (optional)
2 cups cold cooked small pasta (shells, elbows)
1 can (7 ounces) water-packed tuna, drained and broken in chunks
1 cup diagonally sliced celery
2 cups pitted sliced plums, peaches or nectarines
4 cups torn romaine lettuce, rinsed and dried

1. Whisk oil, vinegar, mustard and salt in a large salad bowl until well blended. Add roasted pepper, green onions and garlic, if desired. Stir in pasta, tuna and celery. Cover and marinate at least 30 minutes. (Refrigerate salad if marinating longer.)

2. To serve, add plums and greens. Toss salad well and serve.

Makes 4 servings. Per serving (with plums): 428 calories, 17 grams protein, 28 grams carbohydrate, 28 grams fat, 31 milligrams cholesterol, 348 milligrams sodium

Seafood and Pasta Salad

Lobster, crabmeat and shrimp look-alikes are available in the fresh or frozen seafood section of most supermarkets. For best flavor, look for brands that include a small amount of the actual shellfish with the basic fish (often pollack). This seafood is inexpensive enough to be enjoyed for everyday meals.

    8 ounces snow-peas, trimmed and cut
          crosswise in halves
    8 ounces pasta twists (about 3 cups)
    1 medium-size cucumber, peeled and
          finely chopped
  ½ cup mayonnaise
    2 tablespoons lemon juice
    1 teaspoon dried dillweed
  ¼ teaspoon minced fresh garlic
  12 ounces salad-style imitation lobster
          or crabmeat
    4 plum tomatoes, cut in eighths

1. Bring a large pot of water to a boil over high heat. Add snow-peas and cook about 30 seconds, until crisp-tender and bright green. Remove with a strainer and cool under cold running water. Drain well.

2. Return water to a boil. Add pasta twists and cook according to package directions, stirring frequently, until firm to the bite. Drain in a colander and cool under cold running water. Shake to remove excess water.

3. Mix cucumber, mayonnaise, lemon juice, dill-weed and garlic in a large bowl until blended.

4. Add seafood, snow-peas and pasta and toss to coat well. Spoon onto 4 plates. Arrange tomatoes around each and serve.

Makes 4 servings. Per serving: 548 calories, 21 grams protein, 65 grams carbohydrate, 24 grams fat, 29 milligrams cholesterol, 1,014 milligrams sodium

Seafood and Pasta Salad

Grains

Americans have discovered that grains, like pasta,
are the basis of nutritious, delicious and economical meals.
Discover these wonderful main dishes made with
rice, corn, barley and wheat.

Romaine-Walnut Risotto

Rice Main Dishes

★ SPECIAL—AND WORTH IT
✳ MICROWAVE

Romaine-Walnut Risotto

A salad of thinly sliced oranges and red onion dressed simply with lemon juice and salt is a refreshing accompaniment. Traditionally, Italian risotto is made with *Arborio* rice, a fat short-grained rice. We've found that converted rice makes an excellent substitute.

    2 tablespoons butter or margarine
    ½ cup thinly sliced green onions
    1 cup uncooked converted white rice
    ½ teaspoon salt
    ¼ teaspoon dried tarragon leaves
    ⅛ teaspoon dried thyme leaves
    ⅛ teaspoon crushed red-pepper flakes
    3¾ cups water
    8 ounces (½ large head) romaine
        lettuce, leaves stacked and cut
        crosswise in 1-inch-wide strips
        (about 8 cups)
    8 ounces Italian or Danish fontina
        cheese or Monterey Jack cheese,
        cut in ½-inch cubes (2 cups)
    ¼ cup chopped walnuts
    3 tablespoons finely chopped
        fresh parsley
    1 tablespoon grated Parmesan cheese

1. Melt 1 tablespoon of the butter in a large heavy saucepan or Dutch oven over medium-high heat. Stir in onions and cook 1 to 3 minutes, until nearly tender. Add rice, salt, tarragon, thyme and crushed red pepper. Stir to mix and coat rice with butter.

2. Pour 1¼ cups of the water into saucepan and bring to a boil. Reduce heat to medium and simmer uncovered 7 to 8 minutes, stirring often, until most of the liquid is absorbed.

3. Stir in another 1¼ cups of the water and simmer 7 to 8 minutes longer, stirring two or three times, until most of the liquid is absorbed.

4. Add remaining 1¼ cups water and simmer 5 to 7 minutes, stirring two or three times, until mixture looks creamy and rice is tender but firm.

5. Stir in lettuce. Reduce heat to low. Cover and simmer 2 to 3 minutes, until lettuce wilts.

6. Remove from heat. Stir in fontina cheese, walnuts, parsley and Parmesan. Let stand covered 2 to 3 minutes, just until cheese melts. Spoon into a large heated serving bowl or serve from saucepan.

Makes 4 servings. Per serving: 500 calories, 19 grams protein, 42 grams carbohydrate, 28 grams fat, 75 milligrams cholesterol with butter, 57 milligrams cholesterol with margarine, 658 milligrams sodium

Microwave Method: Reduce amount of water to 2½ cups. Microwave butter and green onions uncovered in a 3-quart microwave-safe bowl on high 1½ to 2 minutes, until onions are nearly tender. Add rice, salt, tarragon, thyme and crushed red pepper. Stir to coat rice with butter. Stir in 1¼ cups of the water. Microwave uncovered on high 9 to 11 minutes, stirring three times, until rice has absorbed almost all the liquid. Add remaining 1¼ cups water. Continue to microwave as directed until most of the water is absorbed. Stir in lettuce. Microwave uncovered on high 1½ to 2 minutes, until lettuce has wilted. Stir in remaining ingredients. Cover and let stand 2 to 3 minutes to melt cheese. Serve.

How Much? How Long?

☐ 1 cup uncooked brown rice, 2½ cups liquid: cook 45–50 minutes, yields 3–4 cups

☐ 1 cup uncooked converted (parboiled) rice, 2½ cups liquid: cook 20–25 minutes, yields 3–4 cups

☐ 1 cup long-grain white rice, 2 cups liquid: cook 15 minutes, yields 3 cups

Risotto with Chicken Livers

Adding extra liquid and stirring during cooking gives the rice a creamy texture, a characteristic of risotto.

- 3 slices bacon
- 12 ounces chicken livers, cut in quarters and trimmed
- 1¼ cups uncooked converted long-grain white rice
- 1 cup sliced green onions
- ½ teaspoon poultry seasoning
- 2½ cups chicken broth mixed with 1 cup water
- ¼ cup grated Parmesan cheese

1. Fry bacon in a large skillet over medium heat until lightly browned and crisp. Remove to paper towels to drain. Drain off all but 1 tablespoon drippings from skillet.

2. Raise heat under skillet to medium-high. Add chicken livers and cook 2 minutes, stirring constantly, just until browned. Remove to a small bowl with a slotted spoon.

3. Add rice, green onions and poultry seasoning to skillet, stirring to coat rice. Pour in 1¼ cups of the broth mixture and bring to a boil. Reduce heat to medium. Simmer 7 to 8 minutes, stirring often, until most of the liquid is absorbed.

4. Stir another 1¼ cups of the broth mixture into rice and simmer 7 to 8 minutes, stirring two or three times, until most of the liquid is absorbed.

5. Add chicken livers with any juices that have accumulated in the bowl and remaining 1 cup broth mixture. Gently stir to mix. Cook 5 to 6 minutes longer, stirring two or three times, until the mixture looks creamy, livers are no longer pink in centers and the rice is tender but firm.

6. Remove from heat. Stir in Parmesan. Spoon risotto onto a heated serving platter and crumble bacon over top. Serve immediately with extra Parmesan cheese to sprinkle over each portion, if desired.

Makes 4 servings. Per serving (without additional cheese): 423 calories, 32 grams protein, 53 grams carbohydrate, 8 grams fat, 653 milligrams cholesterol, 532 milligrams sodium

Risotto with Ham and Vegetables

Made the traditional Italian way; the liquid is added in parts and the rice is stirred often as it cooks.

- 1 tablespoon olive oil
- 12 ounces small mushrooms, quartered (about 3½ cups)
- 1 cup frozen or fresh chopped onion
- 1 teaspoon minced fresh garlic
- 1½ cups uncooked converted long-grain white rice
- 2 cups chicken broth, mixed with 1½ cups water
- 1 box (10 ounces) frozen baby broccoli spears, partially thawed and separated
- 12 ounces fully cooked ham, cut in ½-inch pieces (2 cups)
- 1 tablespoon chopped fresh basil leaves or 1 teaspoon dried basil
- 1 large ripe fresh tomato, cut in ½-inch pieces (about 1 cup)
- ¾ cup grated Parmesan cheese

1. Heat oil in a Dutch oven over medium-high heat. Add mushrooms, onion and garlic. Cook 3 to 4 minutes, stirring often, until mushrooms just start to release their liquid. Remove to a plate with a slotted spoon.

2. Add rice and 1½ cups of the broth mixture to Dutch oven and bring to a boil. Simmer uncovered 8 to 9 minutes, stirring often, until most of the liquid is absorbed.

3. Stir in another 1½ cups of the broth mixture and bring to a boil. Simmer 8 to 9 minutes, stirring two or three times, until most of the liquid is absorbed.

4. Stir in broccoli, mushroom mixture with any juices that have accumulated on the plate and remaining ½ cup broth mixture. Cook about 4 minutes, stirring twice, until broccoli is thawed.

5. Stir in ham and basil. Cook about 3 minutes longer, until mixture looks creamy, most of the liquid is absorbed, ham and broccoli are hot and rice is tender but firm.

6. Remove from heat. Stir in tomato and Parmesan and serve immediately from Dutch oven.

Makes 4 servings. Per serving: 601 calories, 35 grams protein, 71 grams carbohydrate, 19 grams fat, 101 milligrams cholesterol, 1,279 milligrams sodium

Cajun Rice, Chicken and Vegetables

Removing the skin from the chicken reduces the fat by about 50 percent. Spices are cooked briefly in the hot oil because this brings out their flavor.

 2 tablespoons olive oil
 8 chicken thighs (about 2½ pounds), skin and visible fat removed
 1 tablespoon Cajun or Creole seasoning
 ½ teaspoon ground cumin
 1 cup frozen or fresh chopped onion
 1 cup sliced celery
 1½ cups uncooked converted long-grain white rice (brown rice directions follow)
 1 package (10 ounces) frozen chopped collard or mustard greens, thawed and squeezed dry
 2 cups chicken broth
 1 cup water
 1 large red or green bell pepper, cut in 1-inch chunks (about 1 cup)

1. Heat oil in a Dutch oven, preferably nonstick, over medium-high heat. Add chicken thighs without crowding. Cook about 3 minutes per side, until lightly browned. Remove to a plate.

2. Stir Cajun seasoning and cumin into pan drippings until blended, then add onion and celery. When frozen onion is thawed or fresh onion is tender, add rice and greens. Stir in broth and water.

3. Arrange chicken thighs meaty side up in Dutch oven in a single layer. Scatter bell pepper over chicken. Bring to a boil and reduce heat to low. Cover and simmer 23 to 25 minutes, until rice is tender, chicken is no longer pink near the bone and most of the liquid is absorbed. Remove from heat. Let stand covered 5 minutes until all the liquid is absorbed before serving.

Makes 4 servings. Per serving: 529 calories, 35 grams protein, 68 grams carbohydrate, 13 grams fat, 86 milligrams cholesterol, 499 milligrams sodium

Note: If using brown rice: Increase water to 2 cups. Brown chicken and remove to a plate. Stir seasonings and onion into drippings. Add 1½ cups uncooked long-grain brown rice, broth and water. Bring to a boil. Reduce heat to low. Cover and simmer 22 minutes. Stir in celery and greens; add chicken and pepper. Proceed as directed.

Brown Rice versus White Rice

☐ Only the inedible outer hull is removed from brown rice, leaving the bran layer. It takes longer to cook than white rice but contains more nutrients. Light tan in color, it has a chewy texture and nutty flavor.

☐ Regular white rice is the most common kind; the bran layer has been milled away. Some lost nutrients are replaced in a special coating; don't wash the rice or you'll wash away the nutrients.

☐ Parboiled or converted brown or white rice goes through a special steam-pressure process that allows it to retain more nutrients than regular white rice. (Do not confuse it with instant or precooked rice.)

Cajun Rice, Chicken and Vegetables

Beefed-Up Rice with Lima Beans and Okra

Beefed-Up Rice with Lima Beans and Okra

    1 pound lean ground beef
 1½ tablespoons Worcestershire sauce
    1 teaspoon garlic powder
    2 teaspoons olive or vegetable oil
 1½ cups uncooked converted long-
        grain white rice (brown rice
        directions follow)
 2½ cups beef broth
    ½ cup water
    1 box (10 ounces) frozen baby
        lima beans
    1 box (10 ounces) frozen cut okra,
        partially thawed and separated
    ⅓ cup chopped fresh cilantro
    ¼ teaspoon ground red pepper
    ¾ cup sliced green onions

1. Mix beef, Worcestershire sauce and garlic powder in a small bowl until blended.

2. Heat oil in a Dutch oven over high heat. Add beef mixture and cook, stirring to break up large chunks, until meat is no longer pink. Remove to a plate with a slotted spoon.

3. Add rice to Dutch oven and stir to coat with pan drippings. Add broth and water and bring to a boil. Reduce heat to low. Cover and simmer 15 minutes.

4. Stir in lima beans, okra, cilantro and ground red pepper. Cover and simmer 5 minutes.

5. Stir in beef mixture and green onions. Cover and simmer 2 minutes, until rice is tender and most of the liquid is absorbed.

6. Remove from heat and let stand covered 3 minutes, until meat is hot and all the liquid is absorbed. Serve from Dutch oven or spoon into a large heated serving bowl.

Makes 4 servings. Per serving: 726 calories, 36 grams protein, 83 grams carbohydrate, 27 grams fat, 92 milligrams cholesterol, 750 milligrams sodium

Note: If using brown rice: Increase water to 1¼ cups. Assemble meat mixture, brown in hot oil and remove to a plate. Stir 1½ cups uncooked long-grain brown rice into drippings. Add broth and water and bring to a boil. Reduce heat to low, cover and simmer 40 minutes. Proceed as directed above.

Rice with Chinese Cabbage and Turkey

Tenderloins are long, slender pieces of very tender meat found along the underside of each half of a turkey breast. They are usually sold two to a package at the fresh-poultry counter.

12 ounces turkey tenderloin, cut in
     1-inch pieces (2 cups)
2½ tablespoons reduced-sodium soy sauce
2 tablespoons vegetable oil
2 large cloves garlic, peeled and
     cracked open with flat side of a
     knife blade
12 ounces Chinese (napa) or savoy
     cabbage, cored, quartered
     lengthwise, then cut crosswise in
     ½-inch pieces (about 3¼ cups)
2 small half-sour pickles (each about
     3 inches long), chopped (about ⅔ cup)
2 cups chicken broth
1 cup water
1½ cups uncooked converted long-
     grain white rice (brown rice
     directions follow)
1 cup frozen corn kernels
1 large red or green bell pepper, cut
     in ¼-inch-wide strips (about 1 cup)
½ cup sliced green onions

1. Mix turkey and soy sauce in a small bowl.

2. Heat oil and garlic in a Dutch oven over medium-high heat. Cook 2 to 3 minutes, until garlic is golden. Discard garlic.

3. Add turkey to Dutch oven and cook 2 to 3 minutes, stirring constantly, until no longer pink on the outside. Remove to a bowl with a slotted spoon.

4. Add cabbage and pickles to Dutch oven and stir-fry 2 minutes. Put in bowl with turkey.

5. Add broth, water and rice to Dutch oven and bring to a boil. Reduce heat to low. Cover and simmer 10 minutes. Stir in corn and bell pepper. Cover and simmer 8 minutes longer.

6. Return turkey-cabbage mixture to Dutch oven, then stir in green onions. Cover and simmer 5 minutes longer, until most of the liquid is absorbed and turkey is no longer pink in the center when tested with a knife.

7. Remove from heat and let stand covered 3 minutes until all the liquid is absorbed. Serve from Dutch oven or spoon into a large heated serving bowl.

Makes 4 servings. Per serving: 548 calories, 38 grams protein, 73 grams carbohydrate, 11 grams fat, 72 milligrams cholesterol, 970 milligrams sodium

Note: If using brown rice: Increase water to 2 cups. Assemble turkey, soy sauce, oil, garlic, cabbage and pickles as directed. Remove to a bowl. Add broth, water and 1½ cups uncooked long-grain brown rice to Dutch oven. When boiling, reduce heat to low, cover and simmer 35 minutes. Proceed as directed above.

Shrimp and Sausage Paella

A favorite rice dish with a Spanish flair. You can also make this with sweet Italian sausage or breakfast-sausage links.

1 tablespoon olive oil
8 ounces (about 3 links) hot Italian
     sausage, cut in ½-inch-thick rounds
1½ cups uncooked converted long-grain white
     rice (brown rice directions follow)
1 cup frozen or fresh chopped onion
1 teaspoon ground turmeric
2 cups chicken broth
⅓ cup bottled clam juice or water
1 can (16 ounces) stewed tomatoes
½ cup dry white wine or additional
     bottled clam juice
12 jumbo shrimp (about 12 ounces),
     shelled (leave tails on if desired),
     deveined, rinsed and patted dry
1 cup frozen green peas
⅓ cup chopped fresh parsley

1. Heat oil in a Dutch oven over medium-high heat. Add sausage and cook 3 minutes, stirring constantly, until browned on all sides. Remove to a plate with a slotted spoon.

2. Stir rice, onion and turmeric into Dutch oven. Cook about 1 minute, until frozen onion is thawed, or a few minutes longer for fresh onion, until tender. Add broth, clam juice, tomatoes and wine and bring to a boil. Reduce heat to low; cover and simmer 22 minutes.

3. Uncover, stir in browned sausage, shrimp, peas and parsley. Cover and simmer 6 to 8 minutes, until rice is tender, most of the liquid is absorbed and shrimp are pink and opaque. Remove from heat. Serve from Dutch oven or spoon into a large heated serving bowl.

Makes 4 servings. Per serving (with wine): 626 calories, 36 grams protein, 73 grams carbohydrate, 19 grams fat, 170 milligrams cholesterol, 1,218 milligrams sodium

Note: If using brown rice: Increase broth to 2⅓ cups. Brown sausage and remove to a plate. Add 1½ cups uncooked long-grain brown rice, onion and turmeric as directed, then broth, clam juice, tomatoes and wine. When liquid boils, reduce heat to low. Cover and simmer 38 minutes. Stir in sausage and proceed as directed above.

Tex-Mex One-Pot

The "taste of Texas" in an easy rice dish. Adjust the chili powder and hot-pepper sauce to suit your palate.

    3 tablespoons vegetable oil
    1 large onion, chopped (about 1 cup)
    1 large green bell pepper, chopped (about 1 cup)
    1 pound lean ground beef
    1 can (15 ounces) tomato sauce
    1 tomato-sauce can water (1⅔ cups)
    1 box (10 ounces) frozen corn kernels
    1 cup uncooked long-grain white rice
    2 tablespoons chili powder
    1 teaspoon ground cumin
    1 teaspoon salt
    ½ teaspoon pepper
    2 drops hot-pepper sauce
    1 cup shredded extra-sharp Cheddar cheese (4
      ounces)

1. Heat oil in a large saucepan or Dutch oven over medium heat. Stir in onion and bell pepper and cook 3 to 5 minutes, until pepper is crisp-tender.

2. Crumble meat into saucepan and raise heat to medium-high. Cook 6 to 8 minutes, stirring occasionally, until most of the pink color is gone. Drain off any fat.

3. Stir tomato sauce, water, corn, rice, chili powder, cumin, salt, pepper and hot-pepper sauce into saucepan. Bring to a boil. Reduce heat to low. Cover and simmer 18 to 20 minutes, until rice is tender and mixture has thickened.

4. Stir cheese into rice. Cover and cook 2 minutes longer, just until cheese melts. Spoon into a large heated serving bowl and serve immediately.

Makes 4 generous servings. Per serving: 727 calories, 35 grams protein, 66 grams carbohydrate, 37 grams fat, 105 milligrams cholesterol, 1,497 milligrams sodium

Green-Tomato Rice

An easy one-dish supper and a delicious way to make use of green tomatoes from the garden.

    1 tablespoon butter, margarine or vegetable oil
    1 medium-size green tomato, chopped
    1 tablespoon chopped fresh parsley
    1 tablespoon chopped onion
    1 cup uncooked long-grain white rice
   12 ounces smoked sausage, cut in 1-inch pieces
    2 cups chicken broth

1. Heat oven to 350°F.

2. Melt butter over medium heat in a deep 2½-quart ovenproof casserole. Add tomato, parsley and onion and cook about 3 minutes, stirring occasionally. Stir in rice and sausage. Add broth and bring to a boil. Remove from heat.

3. Cover casserole tightly and bake about 40 minutes, until rice is tender and liquid absorbed. Let stand 5 minutes and serve.

Makes 4 servings. Per serving: 508 calories, 18 grams protein, 40 grams carbohydrate, 30 grams fat, 69 milligrams cholesterol with butter, 60 milligrams cholesterol with margarine or vegetable oil, 1,215 milligrams sodium

Fried Rice Dinner

A great way to use up leftover brown or white rice.

    5 tablespoons vegetable oil
    3 cups shredded cabbage
    1¼ cups coarsely shredded carrots
    1 large onion, halved lengthwise and
      thinly sliced
    3 cups cooked white or brown rice
    3 large eggs, beaten
    1½ cups slivered cooked chicken, pork
      or luncheon meat
    ⅓ cup soy sauce
    ⅛ teaspoon pepper
    ½ cup sliced green onions

1. Heat 3 tablespoons of the oil in a large skillet or wok over high heat until very hot but not smoking. Add cabbage, carrots and onion and stir-fry 7 minutes, until crisp-tender. Remove to a bowl with a slotted spoon.

2. Heat remaining 2 tablespoons oil in skillet. Add rice and cook 2 minutes, stirring constantly, until hot.

3. Reduce heat to medium. Make a well in center of rice and pour in eggs. Cook 3 minutes without stirring.

4. Break the soft-cooked eggs into small pieces with a spoon and mix into rice. Add vegetables, chicken, soy sauce and pepper. Toss 2 to 3 minutes, until heated through and eggs are completely cooked. Sprinkle green onions on top and serve immediately.

Makes 4 generous servings. Per serving (with chicken): 530 calories, 28 grams protein, 51 grams carbohydrate, 24 grams fat, 185 milligrams cholesterol, 2,438 milligrams sodium

Creole-Style Rice

Instead of pork, you can use chicken, beef or a combination of meats in this savory dish. Serve with broccoli, spinach or a salad.

2 tablespoons vegetable oil
1 pound lean boneless pork shoulder, cut in ¾-inch pieces
1 large onion, chopped (about 1 cup)
1 medium-size green bell pepper, coarsely chopped (about 1 cup)
1 medium-size fresh tomato, coarsely chopped (about 1 cup)
1 teaspoon minced fresh garlic
2 teaspoons salt
½ teaspoon dried thyme leaves
½ teaspoon pepper
4 cups water
1 box (10 ounces) frozen black-eyed peas or 1 can (16 ounces) red kidney beans or pinto beans, drained
2 cups uncooked converted long-grain white rice
1 tablespoon butter or margarine

1. Heat oil in a Dutch oven over medium-high heat. Add pork without crowding and cook 4 to 5 minutes, stirring often, to brown all sides.

2. Stir onion, bell pepper, tomato, garlic, salt, thyme and pepper into Dutch oven. Cook 4 to 5 minutes, stirring often, until onion is nearly tender. Add water and black-eyed peas and bring to a boil.

3. Stir in rice. Reduce heat to medium-low. Cover and simmer 20 to 25 minutes, until meat and rice are tender and water is absorbed.

4. Remove from heat. Stir in butter; spoon into a heated serving dish and serve.

Makes 6 servings. Per serving: 580 calories, 21 grams protein, 65 grams carbohydrate, 25 grams fat, 53 milligrams cholesterol with butter, 47 milligrams cholesterol with margarine, 809 milligrams sodium

Rice-Vegetable-Tuna Pilaf

Prepare the vegetables while the rice simmers.

2 tablespoons vegetable oil
1 teaspoon minced fresh garlic (optional)
1 cup uncooked long-grain white rice
3 cups chicken broth
1 cup sliced celery
2 green onions, sliced
1 cup thawed frozen or fresh green peas
1 can (12½ ounces) tuna, drained and broken in chunks
1 large fresh tomato, cut in wedges
Pepper to taste
Grated Parmesan cheese (optional)

1. Heat oil in a large heavy skillet over medium heat. Add garlic, if desired, and cook 1 minute. Add rice and cook about 2 minutes, stirring constantly, until rice is translucent.

2. Stir in 2 cups of the chicken broth and bring to a boil. Reduce heat to low. Cover and simmer 10 minutes, until most of the liquid is absorbed.

3. Add remaining 1 cup broth, the celery and green onions. Cover and simmer 5 minutes. Fold peas and tuna into rice. Cover and simmer 5 minutes longer.

4. Remove from heat and let stand 5 minutes. Garnish with tomato wedges. Season with pepper and Parmesan, if desired, and serve.

Makes 4 servings. Per serving (without cheese): 409 calories, 34 grams protein, 48 grams carbohydrate, 8 grams fat, 72 milligrams cholesterol, 669 milligrams sodium

---

Storing Rice

☐ Uncooked regular white and parboiled (converted) white rice keep indefinitely without refrigeration. Once a package is opened, transfer rice to an airtight container.

☐ Because of the oil in its bran layers, brown rice has a shelf life of only about six months; this can be stretched to a year by storing the rice in the refrigerator or freezer.

☐ Plain cooked rice can be stored in the refrigerator for up to one week or in the freezer for six months.

Salmon-Rice Casserole

✳ MICROWAVE
Salmon-Rice Casserole

  3 tablespoons butter or margarine
  ¼ cup all-purpose flour
  ¼ teaspoon salt
  ⅛ teaspoon pepper
  2 cups milk
1½ cups shredded Cheddar cheese
    (6 ounces)
  2 cups cooked Microwave Long-Grain
    White Rice (recipe on page 121)
  1 can (15½ ounces) salmon, drained
    and broken in small chunks
  ⅛ teaspoon ground red pepper
  ¼ teaspoon paprika
For garnish: chopped fresh parsley

1. Put butter in a deep 2-quart microwave-safe casserole. Microwave on high 30 to 60 seconds, until melted. Stir in flour, salt and pepper until smooth. Gradually stir in milk.

2. Microwave on high 5 to 6 minutes, stirring twice. Microwave 2 to 4 minutes longer, stirring every 30 seconds, until thickened. Let cool slightly. Stir in cheese until melted.

3. Stir rice, salmon and ground red pepper into sauce. Sprinkle top with paprika. Microwave on medium-high 4 to 6 minutes, until heated through. Sprinkle with chopped parsley and serve.

Makes 6 servings. Per serving: 395 calories, 24 grams protein, 25 grams carbohydrate, 21 grams fat, 79 milligrams cholesterol with butter, 61 milligrams cholesterol with margarine, 887 milligrams sodium

♥ LOW-CALORIE
Kale, Rice and Cheese Casserole

Try this with corn bread or muffins and a salad of shredded carrots and zucchini.

  2 tablespoons vegetable oil
  1 cup chopped onion
  3 large eggs
  1 cup shredded mild Cheddar cheese
    (4 ounces)
  2 cups cooked long-grain white rice
1½ cups milk
  1 box (10 ounces) frozen chopped
    kale, thawed and drained
  1 teaspoon dried marjoram leaves
  1 teaspoon salt
  ¼ teaspoon pepper

1. Heat oven to 350°F. Grease a deep 2-quart casserole.

2. Heat oil in a small skillet over medium heat. Add onion and cook 5 minutes, stirring occasionally, until wilted.

3. Lightly beat eggs in a large bowl. Stir in onion, ¾ cup of the Cheddar, the rice, milk, kale, marjoram, salt and pepper until blended.

4. Pour rice mixture into prepared casserole. Sprinkle the top with remaining ¼ cup Cheddar. Bake 30 to 40 minutes, until slightly puffed and browned on top. Serve immediately.

Makes 6 servings. Per serving: 296 calories, 13 grams protein, 25 grams carbohydrate, 16 grams fat, 123 milligrams cholesterol, 819 milligrams sodium

Rice and Beans

This combination provides a complete low-fat protein.

Curried Rice, Lentils and Vegetables

For a refreshing accompaniment, mix 1 cup each plain low-fat yogurt and diced, seeded, peeled cucumber. Sprinkle with chopped fresh mint, parsley or sliced green onion tops.

- 1 tablespoon olive oil
- 1 tablespoon plus 1 teaspoon curry powder
- ¾ cup dried lentils, picked over and rinsed
- 3½ cups water
- 1 cup apple juice
- 1 tablespoon instant vegetable-broth granules
- 1½ cups uncooked converted long-grain white rice (brown rice directions follow)
- 3 medium-size carrots, peeled and cut in ¼-inch slices
- ¼ cup Zante currants
- ¼ cup chopped dried apple
- 1 small zucchini and 1 yellow summer squash (5 ounces each), halved lengthwise and cut crosswise in ½-inch-thick slices
- ½ cup sliced green onions

1. Heat oil in a Dutch oven over medium-high heat. Stir in curry powder until blended and cook 1 to 2 minutes to develop flavor. Stir in lentils, then add water, apple juice and broth granules and bring to a boil. Reduce heat to medium. Cover and simmer 18 minutes.

2. Uncover Dutch oven and stir in rice, carrots, currants and dried apple. Return liquid to a boil. Reduce heat to low, cover and simmer 10 minutes.

3. Uncover Dutch oven and stir in squashes. Cover and simmer 3 to 5 minutes longer, until lentils and rice are tender and most of the liquid is absorbed. Remove from heat. Let stand covered 5 minutes, until all the liquid is absorbed. Sprinkle with green onions and serve.

Makes 4 servings. Per serving: 526 calories, 16 grams protein, 107 grams carbohydrate, 4 grams fat, 2 milligrams cholesterol, 407 milligrams sodium

Note: If using brown rice: Increase water to 4½ cups. Heat oil and add curry powder as directed. Stir in lentils and 1½ cups uncooked long-grain brown rice, then water, apple juice and broth granules. When liquid boils, reduce heat to low; cover and simmer 25 minutes. Stir in carrots, currants and apple. Proceed as directed.

Curried Rice, Lentils and Vegetables

Spicy Vegetarian Rice and Beans

Delicious with tortilla chips and a watercress and radish salad.

- 3 cups water
- 2 vegetable bouillon cubes or 2 teaspoons instant broth granules
- 1½ cups uncooked brown rice
- 1 can (19 ounces) red kidney beans, rinsed and drained
- 2 cups frozen or fresh chopped onions
- 1 large green bell pepper, coarsely chopped (about 1 cup)
- 1 cup mild salsa (from a jar)
- 1 teaspoon ground cumin
- 1 can (16 ounces) tomatoes, drained, tomatoes coarsely chopped

1. Put water and bouillon cubes in a Dutch oven and bring to a boil over high heat.

2. Stir in rice. When liquid boils again, stir in kidney beans, onions, bell pepper, salsa and cumin and return to a boil.

3. Reduce heat to low. Cover and simmer 45 minutes, until rice is tender and most of the liquid is absorbed. Remove from heat.

4. Stir in tomatoes. Let stand covered 5 minutes. Spoon into bowls and serve.

Makes 6 servings. Per serving: 314 calories, 11 grams protein, 62 grams carbohydrate, 2 grams fat, 1 milligram cholesterol, 337 milligrams sodium

Spicy Vegetarian Rice and Beans

Paella Rice

Cook's tip: It's easy to cut up the tomatoes in the can with kitchen shears.

- ¼ cup vegetable oil
- 1½ cups chopped onions
- 2 teaspoons minced fresh garlic
- 2 cups uncooked long-grain white rice
- 1 can (28 ounces) tomatoes, tomatoes cut up
- 2 cups chicken broth
- 1½ teaspoons salt
- ¼ teaspoon crushed red-pepper flakes
- ½ teaspoon dried oregano leaves
- ¼ teaspoon ground cumin
- 2 cups frozen green peas, rinsed briefly to thaw
- 1 can (20 ounces) chick-peas, drained
- 1 cup pitted ripe olives

1. Heat oil in a deep large heavy skillet over medium-high heat. Add onions and garlic and cook 3 minutes, until onions start to soften.

2. Add rice and reduce heat to medium. Stir 5 minutes, until rice starts to brown. Add tomatoes and their juice, broth, salt, crushed red pepper, oregano and cumin. Cover and bring to a boil. Reduce heat to low and cook 15 minutes.

3. Sprinkle green peas, chick-peas and olives over rice and press down slightly. Cover and simmer 5 to 10 minutes longer, until liquid is absorbed and rice is tender. Let stand covered 5 minutes before serving.

Makes 8 servings. Per serving: 376 calories, 10 grams protein, 59 grams carbohydrate, 11 grams fat, 4 milligrams cholesterol, 900 milligrams sodium

Savory Black Beans and Rice

Savory Black Beans and Rice

Serve with a salad of sliced oranges or pink grapefruit sections sprinkled with sunflower seeds on a bed of escarole or curly endive. Black beans are sometimes called turtle beans.

2 cups water
½ teaspoon salt
2 cups 5-minute rice
1 tablespoon vegetable oil
½ cup frozen or fresh chopped onion
½ teaspoon minced fresh garlic
2 cans (16 ounces each) black beans, undrained
1 teaspoon poultry seasoning
One 2-inch-long bay leaf
½ teaspoon ground cumin
For garnish: lemon slices and
    parsley sprigs

1. Bring water and salt to a boil in a medium-size saucepan over high heat. Stir in rice. Cover, remove from heat and set aside.

2. Meanwhile, heat oil in another medium-size saucepan over medium heat. Add onion and garlic and cook 2 minutes, until frozen onion is thawed and nearly tender (fresh onion may take a minute or two longer).

3. Stir in black beans and their liquid, poultry seasoning, bay leaf and cumin. Bring to a boil. Reduce heat to low. Cover and simmer 8 to 10 minutes, until heated through and flavors have blended.

4. Remove from heat. Discard bay leaf.

5. Spoon rice onto plates and spoon the bean mixture over the rice. Garnish each serving with a lemon slice and a parsley sprig.

Makes 4 servings. Per serving: 449 calories, 19 grams protein, 83 grams carbohydrate, 5 grams fat, 0 milligrams cholesterol, 283 milligrams sodium

Rice on the Side

Fried Rice with Shiitake Mushrooms

Available fresh year-round, shiitake mushrooms have light- to dark-brown firm-textured caps and add a pleasant smoky flavor to a dish. You can eat the crunchy stems of small young shiitake; discard fibrous stems of larger ones. Substitute white button mushrooms if you prefer.

> ¼ cup butter or margarine
> ½ cup chopped onion
> 1½ cups uncooked converted long-grain white rice
> 1½ cups beef broth
> 1½ cups water
> 4 ounces fresh shiitake mushrooms, stems removed and caps sliced thin (about 2 cups)

1. Melt butter in a medium-size saucepan over medium heat. Add onion and cook 2 to 3 minutes, stirring frequently, until onion is nearly tender. Stir in rice and cook 2 to 3 minutes, stirring constantly, until it starts to brown.

2. Pour broth and water into saucepan. Bring mixture to a boil. Reduce heat, cover and simmer 15 minutes.

3. Uncover saucepan and stir in mushrooms. Cover and simmer 5 minutes longer, until most of the liquid is absorbed and the rice is tender.

4. Remove from heat and let stand covered 5 minutes, until all the liquid is absorbed. Fluff with a fork and serve.

Makes 8 servings. Per serving: 193 calories, 4 grams protein, 30 grams carbohydrate, 6 grams fat, 22 milligrams cholesterol with butter, 4 milligrams cholesterol with margarine, 198 milligrams sodium

Rice with Greens

A soothing dish, good with ham or roast pork or with a bowl of split-pea soup.

> 1 slice bacon, cut in ½-inch pieces
> 1 cup chopped onion
> 2½ cups chicken broth
> 1 box (10 ounces) frozen collard, kale, turnip or mustard greens
> 1½ cups uncooked converted long-grain white rice

1. Fry bacon in a large heavy saucepan over medium-high heat until crisp.

2. Stir onion into saucepan and cook 5 to 6 minutes, stirring often, until golden.

3. Pour broth into saucepan and bring to a boil. Add greens and cook 3 to 4 minutes, stirring occasionally, until thawed and separated.

4. Add rice and return to a boil. Reduce heat to medium-low. Cover and simmer 20 to 25 minutes, until rice is tender but firm and liquid is absorbed. Spoon into a heated medium-size serving dish and serve.

Makes 6 servings, 6 cups. Per serving: 202 calories, 6 grams protein, 37 grams carbohydrate, 3 grams fat, 3 milligrams cholesterol, 471 milligrams sodium

Spanish Rice

Serve this tasty side dish with roast chicken or broiled pork chops. This recipe makes a big batch of rice, so prepare it when you're expecting a crowd for dinner.

> 3 large fresh tomatoes, peeled (see Peeling Tomatoes, page 10), or 1 can (28 ounces) tomatoes, drained
> 1 cup chopped onion
> 1 large clove garlic
> ½ teaspoon ground cumin
> ¼ teaspoon pepper
> ¼ cup vegetable oil
> 2 cups uncooked long-grain converted white rice
> 3¼ cups chicken broth
> ½ teaspoon salt, or to taste
> ¼ cup chopped fresh parsley

1. Put tomatoes, onion, garlic, cumin and pepper in a food processor or a blender. Process until smooth.

2. Heat oil in a large heavy skillet (not one with a nonstick coating) over medium heat. Add rice and stir quickly to coat with oil. Cook 7 to 10 minutes, stirring often, until rice is browned.

3. Stir tomato mixture, broth and salt into skillet. Cover and bring to a boil. Reduce heat to low and simmer 20 minutes.

4. Uncover skillet and sprinkle rice with parsley. Cover and simmer 10 minutes longer, until all the liquid is absorbed. Let stand 5 minutes before serving.

Makes 12 generous servings, 8 cups. Per serving: 174 calories, 4 grams protein, 29 grams carbohydrate, 5 grams fat, 4 milligrams cholesterol, 289 milligrams sodium

✳ MICROWAVE
Microwave Long-Grain White Rice

For successful results, microwave rice in a microwave-safe bowl or casserole dish twice the height of the rice and liquid to prevent boil-overs. Cover dish tightly with a lid or vented plastic wrap. Be sure to let rice stand after cooking so that any remaining liquid will be absorbed and rice will be dry and fluffy.

1½ cups water
1 teaspoon vegetable oil
½ teaspoon salt
⅔ cup uncooked long-grain white rice

1. Mix water, oil and salt in a deep 1-quart microwave-safe casserole or bowl. Stir in rice. Cover tightly with a lid or vented plastic wrap. Microwave on high 4 to 7 minutes, until water starts to boil.

2. Reduce power to medium. Microwave 10 to 12 minutes longer, until rice is tender and most of the liquid is absorbed. Let stand covered 3 to 5 minutes, until all the liquid is absorbed. Fluff with a fork. Serve as a side dish or use in Salmon-Rice Casserole (recipe on page 116).

Makes 2 cups. Per ½ cup: 112 calories, 2 grams protein, 25 grams carbohydrate, 1 gram fat, 0 milligrams cholesterol, 268 milligrams sodium

✳ MICROWAVE
Rice Pilaf

Although cooking rice in the microwave may not save time, it can certainly cut cleanup since you can cook, serve, then store and even reheat left-overs in the same dish.

1 medium-size onion, coarsely chopped (about ½ cup)
1 large stalk celery, coarsely chopped (about ½ cup)
1½ tablespoons butter or margarine
4 ounces mushrooms, thinly sliced (about 2 cups)
1¾ cups chicken broth
1 cup uncooked long-grain white rice
1 tablespoon chopped fresh parsley

1. Put onion, celery and butter in a deep 2-quart microwave-safe casserole. Microwave on high 2 to 4 minutes, until vegetables are crisp-tender.

2. Stir in mushrooms, broth and rice. Cover with a lid or vented plastic wrap. Microwave on high 4 to 6 minutes, until liquid boils.

3. Reduce power to medium. Microwave 15 to 25 minutes, until the liquid is absorbed.

4. Carefully remove lid and stir in parsley. Cover and let stand 5 minutes before serving.

Makes about 3½ cups. Per ½ cup: 134 calories, 3 grams protein, 24 grams carbohydrate, 3 grams fat, 11 milligrams cholesterol with butter, 3 milligrams cholesterol with margarine, 198 milligrams sodium

Rice Cakes with Cheese and Mushrooms

Serve these cakes as a side dish or with a salad or green vegetable for a pleasant light supper.

3 cups cooked long-grain white rice
3 large eggs
1 cup cottage cheese
6 tablespoons chopped fresh parsley
6 tablespoons grated Parmesan or Romano cheese
½ teaspoon salt
¼ teaspoon pepper
½ cup packaged dry bread crumbs
About ½ cup vegetable oil
2 tablespoons butter or margarine
4 ounces mushrooms, sliced (about 2 cups)
½ teaspoon minced fresh garlic

1. Mix rice, 1 of the eggs, the cottage cheese, 3 tablespoons *each* of the parsley and Parmesan, the salt and pepper in a large bowl until well blended.

2. Beat remaining 2 eggs in a shallow dish. Mix bread crumbs and remaining 3 tablespoons *each* parsley and cheese on a sheet of waxed paper.

3. Shape rice mixture into twelve 3-inch patties about 1 inch thick. Dip in beaten eggs, letting excess egg drip off, then coat in bread-crumb mixture. Chill on a baking sheet 30 minutes.

4. Heat 2 tablespoons of the oil in a large skillet (preferably nonstick) over medium heat. Cook patties in batches without crowding 3 minutes per side, until golden brown. Add more oil as needed. Transfer cooked patties to a heated platter and keep warm in a low oven.

5. Meanwhile, melt butter in a small skillet over medium heat. Stir in mushrooms and garlic and cook 3 to 4 minutes, until mushrooms are just wilted. Spoon mushroom mixture over rice cakes and serve.

Makes 4 servings. Per serving: 547 calories, 20 grams protein, 50 grams carbohydrate, 28 grams fat, 198 milligrams cholesterol with butter, 180 milligrams cholesterol with margarine, 1,164 milligrams sodium

Corn

Cornmeal, whole hominy and grits are all made from corn. Cornmeal is the whole kernel that has been dried and ground. Hominy is dried corn kernels with the hull and germ removed. It is most often available canned and ready to eat. Grits are ground dried corn with the hull and germ removed.

🕐 **MAKE-AHEAD**
✳ **MICROWAVE**

Chile-Cheese Polenta with Salsa

Accompany this with a crisp green salad dressed with oil and vinegar. Polenta and salsa can be made up to two days ahead, and the whole dish can be assembled, covered and refrigerated up to one day ahead.

4 cups skim milk
1 cup yellow cornmeal
1 teaspoon salt
¼ teaspoon pepper
1 can (4 ounces) chopped green chiles, undrained
1 cup shredded Monterey Jack cheese (4 ounces)
⅓ cup grated Parmesan cheese
Salsa (recipe follows)

1. Lightly grease a 13x9x2-inch baking pan.

2. Mix milk, cornmeal, salt and pepper in a medium-size heavy saucepan. Bring to a boil over medium-high heat, stirring often with a wooden spoon. Reduce heat to low and simmer 5 to 6 minutes, stirring often, until smooth and thick. Remove from heat.

3. Stir chiles and their liquid into cornmeal mixture. Spread evenly in prepared pan. Refrigerate uncovered at least 1 hour, until firm. (If refrigerating longer, cover well to prevent drying.)

4. Heat oven to 400°F. Lightly grease a 9- to 10-inch round shallow baking dish.

5. To assemble: Cut chilled polenta into twenty-four 2-inch squares. Arrange squares in prepared baking dish in slightly overlapping rows of diamonds. Sprinkle with Monterey Jack and Parmesan cheeses.

6. Cover loosely with foil and bake 15 minutes. Remove foil and bake 10 to 15 minutes longer, until edges begin to brown. Cool in pan on rack about 10 minutes. Spoon the salsa over polenta and serve.

Makes 6 servings. Per serving (with ¼ cup salsa): 308 calories, 15 grams protein, 32 grams carbohydrate, 13 grams fat, 47 milligrams cholesterol, 670 milligrams sodium

Microwave Method: Increase cornmeal to 1¼ cups. Mix milk, cornmeal, salt and pepper in a 2-quart microwave-safe bowl. Microwave uncovered on high 10 to 12 minutes, stirring every 3 minutes, until mixture is smooth and thick. Stir in chiles and chill as directed. Assemble in a microwave-safe baking dish as directed. Microwave uncovered on high 5 to 6 minutes, rotating dish ¼ turn every 2 minutes, until polenta is hot and cheeses just begin to melt. Let stand 5 minutes.

Salsa

1½ cups coarsely chopped ripe fresh tomatoes
¼ cup thinly sliced green onions
¼ cup chopped fresh cilantro leaves
1 tablespoon lime juice
1 teaspoon minced fresh or canned jalapeño pepper
¼ teaspoon salt

1. Mix all ingredients in a small bowl; cover and refrigerate. Bring to room temperature before serving. Serve with Chile-Cheese Polenta (recipe above).

Makes 1½ cups.

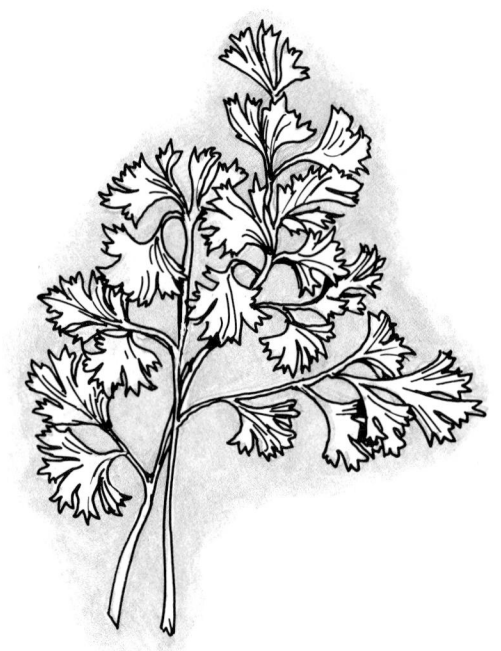

Chile-Cheese Polenta with Salsa

✳ MICROWAVE

Polenta

Polenta is a cousin to our own Southern corn-meal mush. Serve with a hearty beef or veal stew. For a light dinner or brunch, sprinkle polenta with coarsely grated Parmesan cheese and serve with a juicy ripe-tomato salad.

6⅓ cups water
  1 tablespoon salt
  2 cups yellow cornmeal

1. Lightly grease a shallow 2- to 3-quart oven-proof bowl.

2. Bring water and salt to a brisk boil in a large heavy saucepan over high heat. Reduce heat to medium-low. Gradually sprinkle in cornmeal, whisking constantly to prevent lumps from forming.

3. Simmer cornmeal 20 to 25 minutes, stirring often with a long-handled wooden spoon until

very thick (the spoon will stand up in cornmeal) but still pourable.

4. Pour and scrape polenta into prepared bowl. Spread level with a rubber spatula or the back of a spoon. Let stand 8 to 10 minutes, until firm to the touch and polenta pulls away from sides of bowl.

5. Invert onto a large serving plate. Slice into wedges and serve.

Makes 6 servings. Per serving: 167 calories, 4 grams protein, 36 grams carbohydrate, 1 gram fat, 0 milligrams cholesterol, 1,099 milligrams sodium

Microwave Method: Whisk all ingredients in a 3-quart microwave-safe bowl. Cover with a lid or vented plastic wrap. Microwave on high 14 to 16 minutes, stirring once, until very thick but still pourable. Scrape down sides of bowl. Let stand uncovered until polenta is firm and pulls away from sides of bowl. Continue as directed above.

Grits, Cheese and Chile Bake

A breakfast favorite in the South, grits belong on the dinner table, too.

- **3 cups water**
- **1 teaspoon salt**
- **¾ cup quick hominy grits**
- **1½ cups shredded Cheddar cheese (6 ounces)**
- **⅓ cup butter or margarine**
- **⅓ cup milk**
- **2 large eggs, lightly beaten**
- **1 can (4 ounces) chopped green chiles, undrained**

1. Heat oven to 375°F. Grease a 1½-quart shallow baking dish.

2. Put water and salt in a large saucepan and bring to a boil over medium-high heat. Slowly stir in grits. Reduce heat to low and cook 5 minutes, stirring occasionally, until thick. Remove from heat.

3. Stir cheese, butter, milk and eggs into grits until cheese melts. Stir in chiles and their juice.

4. Pour into prepared casserole. Bake 30 minutes, until hot and golden. Serve immediately.

Makes 4 servings. Per serving: 473 calories, 17 grams protein, 27 grams carbohydrate, 33 grams fat, 187 milligrams cholesterol with butter, 142 milligrams cholesterol with margarine, 1,055 milligrams sodium

Hominy-Turkey Scramble

Hominy is a staple in Southwest cooking. It is sometimes called posole, which is also the name of a very thick soup made with hominy.

- **3 tablespoons butter or margarine**
- **1 pound ground turkey**
- **1 tablespoon all-purpose flour**
- **½ cup sliced green onions**
- **½ teaspoon dried thyme leaves, or to taste**
- **¼ teaspoon pepper, or to taste**
- **1 can (16 ounces) hominy, well drained**
- **1 cup chicken broth**
- **2 tablespoons soy sauce**
- **1 large carrot, coarsely shredded**

1. Melt butter in a large skillet over medium heat until lightly browned. Add turkey and cook, breaking up with a wooden spoon, just until meat is no longer pink.

2. Stir in flour, green onions, thyme and pepper and cook 2 minutes. Add hominy, broth and soy sauce and cook, stirring constantly, until mixture thickens slightly. Cover and simmer about 5 minutes to blend flavors. Stir in carrot. Remove from heat. Spoon into bowls and serve.

Makes 4 servings. Per serving: 382 calories, 39 grams protein, 21 grams carbohydrate, 16 grams fat, 129 milligrams cholesterol with butter, 102 milligrams cholesterol with margarine, 1,277 milligrams sodium

Hominy-Turkey Scramble

BARLEY

Barley is a hardy cereal grain belonging to the grass family. Pearled barley has had most of the inedible tough outer hull rubbed off so that it cooks more quickly.

✳ MICROWAVE
Barley—Chick-pea Skillet

This satisfying meatless dinner-in-a-skillet goes from range top to the table in under 30 minutes.

      3 cups water
      1 tablespoon minced fresh garlic
    ½ teaspoon salt
    ½ teaspoon dried basil leaves, crumbled
    ¼ teaspoon pepper
  1¼ cups quick-cooking barley
      1 can (10½ ounces) chick-peas,
            drained
    ½ cup small pitted ripe olives,
            chopped
      4 ounces mozzarella cheese, cut in
            ½-inch cubes
      2 small green onions, sliced
            (about ¼ cup)
      4 ounces small fresh spinach leaves,
            thick stems removed, leaves rinsed
            and dried (about 2 cups)
      8 cherry tomatoes, halved
            (about 1 cup)

1. Put water, garlic, salt, basil and pepper in a deep 10-inch skillet over medium-high heat. Bring to a boil.

2. Stir in barley, chick-peas and olives. Return to a boil. Reduce heat to low. Cover and simmer 13 to 15 minutes, until barley is tender and most of the liquid is absorbed.

3. Quickly stir cheese into barley and sprinkle with green onions. Arrange spinach leaves around edge of skillet and top with tomatoes.

4. Cover and cook 2 minutes longer, until spinach is wilted, cheese melted and liquid absorbed. Spoon into a heated serving bowl or serve right from skillet.

Makes 4 servings. Per serving: 415 calories, 16 grams protein, 64 grams carbohydrate, 12 grams fat, 22 milligrams cholesterol, 524 milligrams sodium

Microwave Method: Reduce garlic to ½ teaspoon, basil to ¼ teaspoon and pepper to ⅛ teaspoon. Put in a 3-quart microwave-safe bowl with water. Cover with a lid or vented plastic wrap. Microwave on high 10 to 12 minutes, until boiling. Stir in barley, chick-peas and olives. Cover and microwave on high 13 to 15 minutes, until most of the liquid has been absorbed and barley is tender. Stir in cheese and green onions. Top with spinach and tomatoes. Cover and microwave 30 to 60 seconds, until spinach starts to wilt. Cover and let stand 5 minutes, until liquid is absorbed, spinach wilted and cheese melted.

🕐 MAKE-AHEAD
Mushroom-Barley Casserole

The familiar flavors of mushroom-barley soup baked into a great casserole. Serve with a roast chicken or juicy pork loin. Leftovers may be cooled and frozen. Thaw in refrigerator or microwave oven before using. Reheat in a heavy saucepan with a little water.

      3 tablespoons butter or margarine
      3 tablespoons vegetable oil
      1 pound medium pearled barley
            (about 2¼ cups)
      2 large onions, chopped
            (about 2 cups)
  1½ teaspoons minced fresh garlic
    12 ounces mushrooms, sliced
            (about 6 cups)
  Three 2-inch-long bay leaves
      6 cups chicken broth or water
    ½ teaspoon salt
    ¼ teaspoon pepper

1. Heat butter and oil in a 3-quart range-top-to-oven casserole or Dutch oven over medium heat. Stir in barley, onions and garlic and cook 5 minutes, until onions are nearly tender.

2. Stir in mushrooms and bay leaves and cook 5 minutes, stirring occasionally, until mushrooms are lightly browned. Discard bay leaves.

3. Stir chicken broth, salt and pepper into barley. Raise heat to medium-high and bring to a boil. (This may take about 20 minutes.)

4. Meanwhile, heat oven to 350°F.

5. Cover casserole and bake 45 minutes, until barley is tender. Spoon into a heated serving dish or serve from casserole.

Makes 8 servings. Per serving: 322 calories, 9 grams protein, 51 grams carbohydrate, 10 grams fat, 24 milligrams cholesterol with butter, 10 milligrams cholesterol with margarine, 664 milligrams sodium

Wheat

Bulgur is whole wheat that has been cooked and dried, then cracked into coarse fragments. Farina is coarsely ground wheat with the bran and most of the wheat germ removed.

Bulgur and Vegetable Pilaf

Pair this curry-flavored pilaf with a salad of sliced tomatoes and bell peppers sprinkled with a tangy vinaigrette dressing.

4 cups water
3 vegetable bouillon cubes or
    1 tablespoon instant broth granules
1 tablespoon curry powder
1 teaspoon minced fresh garlic
2 medium-size carrots, coarsely
    shredded (about 1 cup)
2 boxes (10 ounces each) frozen baby
    lima beans (4 cups)
2 cups uncooked bulgur wheat
Sliced green onions and sour cream or
    plain yogurt (optional)

1. Put water, bouillon cubes, curry powder and garlic in a medium-size saucepan. Cover and bring to a boil over high heat.

2. Add carrots, lima beans and bulgur to saucepan. Return to a boil. Reduce heat to low. Cover and simmer 12 minutes, until all the liquid is absorbed and bulgur is tender.

3. Spoon into a heated serving dish. Sprinkle with green onions. Spoon sour cream on top, if desired, and serve.

Makes 4 servings. Per serving (without green onions and sour cream): 588 calories, 24 grams protein, 121 grams carbohydrate, 2 grams fat, 2 milligrams cholesterol, 946 milligrams sodium

Bulgur and Vegetable Pilaf

⏱ MAKE-AHEAD
Farina Gnocchi with Basil Butter

This dish freezes well. Gnocchi are Italian dumplings made from potatoes, semolina flour or, in this case, farina. These make an excellent light supper, served with a big salad or paired with roast lamb.

1½ cups milk
1½ cups water
  1 teaspoon salt
 ¾ cup uncooked quick farina
  3 tablespoons butter or margarine
 ¼ cup plus 1 tablespoon grated
      Parmesan cheese
Basil Butter (recipe follows)

1. Bring milk, water and salt to a boil in a medium-size saucepan. Reduce heat to medium-low and gradually stir in farina. Cook 2 to 3 minutes, stirring constantly with a wooden spoon, until thick. Reduce heat to low, cook and stir another minute or two, until very thick.

2. Add butter and ¼ cup of the Parmesan to farina and stir until butter melts.

3. Spread hot mixture about ½ inch thick on a baking sheet. Let stand until cool and firm, about 20 minutes.

4. Meanwhile, heat oven to 350°F. Grease a shallow baking dish.

5. Using a knife or a round cookie cutter, cut the firm farina mixture into squares, diamonds or circles. (You can knead the trimmings, flatten them and cut more shapes.) Arrange gnocchi in an overlapping pattern in prepared baking dish.

6. Dot with Basil Butter. Sprinkle with remaining 1 tablespoon Parmesan. Bake 30 minutes, until hot and slightly browned. Serve.

Makes 4 servings. Per serving: 385 calories, 9 grams protein, 30 grams carbohydrate, 25 grams fat, 82 milligrams cholesterol with butter, 19 milligrams cholesterol with margarine, 954 milligrams sodium

Basil Butter
¼ cup butter or margarine, at room
    temperature
2 teaspoons crumbled dried basil
½ teaspoon minced fresh garlic

1. Mix all ingredients in a small bowl until well blended. Use as directed in Farina Gnocchi recipe above.

Makes ¼ cup.

Index

127

For information on how you can have
Better Homes and Gardens
delivered to your door, write to:
Mr. Robert Austin
P.O. Box 4536
Des Moines, IA 50336